616.852 Ano
Anorexia /

34028076158493
JC $21.85 ocn535494169
10/13/10

W9-DJB-551

HARRIS COUNTY PUBLIC LIBRARY

At Issue

Anorexia

Other Books in the At Issue Series:

At Issue

Anorexia

Stefan Kiesbye, Book Editor

GREENHAVEN PRESS
A part of Gale, Cengage Learning

GALE
CENGAGE Learning™

Detroit • New York • San Francisco • New Haven, Conn • Waterville, Maine • London

GALE
CENGAGE Learning

Christine Nasso, *Publisher*
Elizabeth Des Chenes, *Managing Editor*

© 2010 Greenhaven Press, a part of Gale, Cengage Learning.

Gale and Greenhaven Press are registered trademarks used herein under license.

For more information, contact:
Greenhaven Press
27500 Drake Rd.
Farmington Hills, MI 48331-3535
Or you can visit our Internet site at gale.cengage.com

ALL RIGHTS RESERVED.
No part of this work covered by the copyright herein may be reproduced, transmitted, stored, or used in any form or by any means graphic, electronic, or mechanical, including but not limited to photocopying, recording, scanning, digitizing, taping, Web distribution, information networks, or information storage and retrieval systems, except as permitted under Section 107 or 108 of the 1976 United States Copyright Act, without the prior written permission of the publisher.

For product information and technology assistance, contact us at

Gale Customer Support, 1-800-877-4253
For permission to use material from this text or product, submit all requests online at www.cengage.com/permissions

Further permissions questions can be e-mailed to permissionrequest@cengage.com

Articles in Greenhaven Press anthologies are often edited for length to meet page requirements. In addition, original titles of these works are changed to clearly present the main thesis and to explicitly indicate the author's opinion. Every effort is made to ensure that Greenhaven Press accurately reflects the original intent of the authors. Every effort has been made to trace the owners of copyrighted material.

Cover Image copyright © Images.com/Corbis.

LIBRARY OF CONGRESS CATALOGING-IN-PUBLICATION DATA

Anorexia / Stefan Kiesbye, book editor.
    p. cm. -- (At issue)
Includes bibliographical references and index.
ISBN 978-0-7377-4866-6 (hardcover) -- ISBN 978-0-7377-4867-3 (pbk.)
1. Anorexia nervosa--Popular works. I. Kiesbye, Stefan.
RC552.A5A5474 2010
616.85'262--dc22
                                                            2010007870

Printed in the United States of America
1 2 3 4 5 6 7 14 13 12 11 10

Contents

Introduction

Although it may be hard to pinpoint exactly when being thin became all the rage in the twentieth century, the rise of supermodel Twiggy in the mid-1960s demonstrates clearly Western culture's changing attitude toward the female body. Twiggy introduced the world to an androgynous look, the use of teenage models, and the perception that no woman could be too thin. Twiggy claims she was never anorexic, and in a 2002 interview with *Good Housekeeping* she says,

> It was so unfair that I got blamed for encouraging anorexia in the Sixties and Seventies. And, yes, I was bruised by it because I didn't feel it was my fault. Magazines that choose only [the] skinniest models are very irresponsible. If teenagers aren't naturally thin like I was, the pressure on them is dangerous.

She claims that she was naturally skinny, but her look became predominant, to the extent that many women started to starve themselves in order to become like her. And even though fashion designers have claimed from time to time that curves will make a comeback, runway models today are as thin as ever. Anorexia, in fact, is so widespread among top models, that several European countries have designed laws to prohibit underweight women from appearing on the catwalk. The deaths of South American models Eliana and Luisel Ramos only underscore the sad track record of the fashion industry.

While extreme pressure on women to adhere to the beauty standards of the time has long been an issue, however, men have not historically been the target of the fashion industry. In popular culture, men are often portrayed as rotund slobs, and in cartoons this stereotypical fashion-challenged man survives even today. In comic strips from *Zits* to *Baby Blues* to

Drabble, fathers are usually beer-bellied men with thinning hair, a bit slow but happy. Their wives are thin, often domineering, and smart.

Yet male anorexia is becoming a serious issue. In a June 25, 2000 article for *The New York Times*, Erica Goode states that research has shown the number of men with eating disorders might be much greater than previously suspected. "In a study of 10,000 residents of Ontario [Canada], for example, University of Toronto researchers found that 1 of every 6 people who qualified for a full or partial diagnosis of anorexia was male—substantially more than the 1 in 10 usually reported in studies of patients in eating-disorder programs." According to Goode, men are less concerned with being thin than with having well-defined muscles. "If the anorexic or bulimic woman's nightmare is being told that she has 'a little meat on her thighs,' many men live in fear of being told that they 'still have a little fat on those delts.'" And because anorexia is labeled as a woman's illness, many men shy away from seeking professional help and avoid consulting with a doctor.

For 19-year-old Chris Hardy, controlling his food intake meant exacting control over his fate. In a 2009 interview with the BBC, he acknowledged that external upheaval led him to become obsessed with his body.

> A lot of stuff happened at 11 or 12 that was quite traumatic. My parents divorced, I moved [to a new] school, moved house. And then you also start to become more aware of body image at that age anyway. ... I would count out the exact number of pieces of cereal to eat to have each morning, have a cracker [at] lunchtime, and then maybe a few bits of pasta in the evening ... It was nothing really, but even that seemed too much and I would work on reducing it the next day. That was how I got a sense of achievement.

In a culture in which image is highly important, and in which body weight is associated with laziness and failure, men and women struggle with perfectionism and low confidence.

Goode writes that "they seek to gain control over their lives by controlling their bodies. They often suffer from depression, anxiety, alcohol or drug abuse or other psychiatric conditions in addition to their eating-related symptoms. Most have a severely distorted image of their bodies, seeing obesity in the mirror where others see skin and bones."

The viewpoints in *At Issue: Anorexia* examine this devastating illness from a variety of perspectives, illuminating issues important to its victims and the people who love them.

1

The Body Image Presented by the Media Promotes Disordered Eating

Jennifer Derenne and Eugene Beresin

Jennifer Derenne is an assistant professor of psychiatry and behavioral medicine at the Medical College of Wisconsin. Eugene Beresin is codirector of the Harvard Medical School Center for Mental Health and Media and the coauthor of the book Child Adolescent Psychiatric Clinics of North America: Child Psychiatry and the Media.

Standards of beauty are constantly changing, are never realistic, and depend heavily on social context. Although this has always been the case, the modern media culture is relentless in advertising ideal figures, represented by male and female supermodels and action heroes. The barrage of images of ultrathin women and extremely muscular men has led to a general dissatisfaction among consumers, and might be a cause of depression, low self-esteem, and eating disorders, such as anorexia. A healthy diet, exercise, and a lifestyle centered on physical activities instead of TV or computer use is essential to create a healthy attitude toward one's body.

Our nation's health has reached a point of crisis. According to the American Obesity Association, 65% of adults and 30% of children are overweight, and 30% of adults and 15% of children meet the criteria for obesity. Rarely playing

Jennifer Derenne and Eugene Beresin, "Body Image, Media, and Eating Disorder," *Academic Psychiatry*, May-June 2006. Copyright © 2006 Academic Psychiatry. All rights reserved. Reproduced by permission.

outdoors, children spend their days chatting online or watching TV while snacking on nutritionally empty foods. The average child spends 4 hours per day watching TV, and only 1 hour per day completing homework. Similarly, the adult workplace has become more and more sedentary.

At the same time, rates of some eating disorders in women, such as anorexia nervosa and bulimia nervosa, are rising, and increasing numbers of men are seeking treatment as well. Patients are being referred at progressively younger ages. There is a significant dichotomy [division into contradictory opinions] between society's idealized rail-thin figure and the more typical American body. The reasons for this are complex and likely involve the interplay of media pressure to be thin, family eating and exercise patterns, and a relative surplus of nonnutritious food. Dietary restriction leads to a repetitive pattern of self-deprivation, which can result in bingeing, weight gain, and worsening self-image.

Although it is tempting to blame today's media for perpetuating and glorifying unrealistic standards of physical beauty, the truth is far more complicated. Throughout history, the dominant political climate and cultural ideals always have shaped the public's perception of the ideal female body type. However, today's culture is unique in that the media (including television, Internet, movies, and print) is a far more powerful presence than ever before. . . .

Ideal Body Type Throughout History

Throughout history, the standard of female beauty often has been unrealistic and difficult to attain. [People] with money and higher socioeconomic status were far more likely to be able to conform to these standards. Women typically were willing to sacrifice comfort and even endure pain to achieve them.

In colonial times, the harsh environment and lack of comfortable surroundings required that all family members contribute to survival. Large families were preferred, as children could help [to tend] the land and [aid with] household chores. For these reasons, communities valued fertile, physically strong and able women. However, in the 19th century, ideals shifted and women with tiny waists and large bustles came to be valued. It was desirable for an upper-class man to be able to span a woman's waist with his hands. If women were too frail to work, plantation owners could justify the use of slaves. Indeed, much emphasis was placed on female fragility, which then made a woman a more attractive candidate for marriage. The ideal wealthy woman of the time was sickly and prone to headaches; the fine art of fainting was taught in finishing schools throughout the country. Women of significant financial means would go as far as having ribs removed to further decrease their waist size. Despite being painful and causing health problems, such as shortness of breath (which could lead to pneumonia) and dislocated visceral organs, corsets became the height of fashion.

Some have said that the invention of the corset was the main impetus for the feminist movement at the beginning of the 20th century. Women turned up their noses at complicated dresses, instead favoring pants, which were comfortable and did not restrict movement. They cut their hair short, bound their breasts, took up cigarette smoking, and fought for the right to vote. At this point, it was fashionable to be angular, thin, and boyish-looking, and manufacturers routinely featured pictures of "flappers" in their advertisements.

During the Second World War, ideals changed yet again. With their husbands overseas, young women went to work so that industry could thrive. In their spare time, some of them formed professional sports teams. Again, society valued competent, strong, and physically able women. However, things changed after the war. The men came home and cultural values shifted again to emphasize traditional family and gender roles. Women took to wearing dresses and skirts. Again highlighting the importance of fertility (this . . . period marked the beginning of the Baby Boom era), the population favored a more curvaceous frame, like that of Marilyn Monroe.

Before awards ceremonies, attendees routinely fast and endure tight-fitting undergarments to flatten their stomachs for unforgiving evening gowns.

In the 1960s, major changes were in the works. Along with people of color, women were again fighting for equality both in the home and in the workplace. The advent of the birth control pill afforded increased sexual freedom; women burned their bras. Similar to the trends found during the suffrage movement at the beginning of the century, women of the decade idealized thin and boyish bodies like that of the emaciated supermodel Twiggy.

Current Media Influence

The current media culture is complicated and very confusing. Women are told that they can and should "have it all." They expect family, career, and home to be perfect, and [style expert] Martha Stewart tells them how to do it. The media inundates them with mixed messages about what is sexy, making it difficult to choose a role model. The heroin chic waif [any young-looking woman whose emaciation was meant to evoke that of drug users] made popular by Kate Moss in the early 1990s competes with the voluptuous *Baywatch* [a 1980's TV series about a group of swimsuit-clad lifeguards] babe personified by Pamela Anderson and the athletic soccer stars who celebrated a World Cup victory by tearing their shirts off. Though it is highly unlikely for a rail-thin woman to have natural DD-cup size breasts, toy manufacturers set this expectation by developing and marketing the Barbie doll, whose measurements are physiologically impossible. Thankfully, Barbie's designers revamped her figure back in the late 1990s.

However, with [the] increased availability of plastic surgery, today's women are faced with similarly unrealistic expectations every time they open a fashion magazine.

In 2002, actress Jamie Lee Curtis famously posed for *More* magazine, both in typical "glammed up" attire and then in her sports bra and shorts. The reality is that most magazines airbrush photos and use expensive computer technology to correct blemishes and hide figure flaws. In fact, in Jamie Lee's own words, she has ". . . very big breasts and a soft, fatty little tummy . . . and . . . back fat." She felt that women should know that the figures portrayed by the media are rarely real. Granted, celebrities can afford to hire personal trainers and nutritionists to assist in their weight-loss endeavors. Stylists select fetching outfits, and tailors wait on standby to make sure that clothes fit like second skin. Before awards ceremonies, attendees routinely fast and endure tight-fitting undergarments to flatten their stomachs for unforgiving evening gowns.

Eating Disorders Are Widespread

Celebrities are no less susceptible to eating disorders than the rest of the population. Mary-Kate Olsen was hospitalized with anorexia nervosa, and the weekly gossip magazines have speculated consistently about the health of Lindsay Lohan and Nicole Richie. Their concern for the well-being of these young women is tainted by additional articles in the same issues of their publications [that] criticize singer-actress Jennifer Lopez's ample bottom and praise supermodel Heidi Klum for being "runway ready" merely 4 weeks after giving birth to her second child. Twenty-five years ago, the average fashion model was 8% thinner than the average woman. Today, that number has risen to 23%, [probably] reflecting a combination of rising obesity rates in the general population and progressively thinner ideals. Even health and fitness magazines are not above scrutiny. Articles tout the importance of moderate diet and exercise, but pages are filled with advertisements for appetite suppressants and diet supplements. The diet industry is a multibillion dollar business. Women are consistently given the message that they are not pretty enough or thin enough.

Excessive media consumption also may be correlated with the rate of childhood depression.

No discussion of body image and the media would be complete without referencing [Anne] Becker's landmark study comparing rates of eating disorders before and after the arrival of television in Fiji in 1995. Ethnic Fijians have traditionally encouraged healthy appetites and have preferred a more rotund body type, which signified wealth and the ability to care for one's family. Strong cultural identity is thought to be protective against eating disorders; there was only one case of anorexia nervosa reported on the island prior to 1995. However, in 1998, rates of dieting skyrocketed from 0% to 69%, and young people routinely cited the appearance of the attractive actors on shows like *Beverly Hills 90210* and *Melrose Place* as the inspiration for their weight loss. For the first time, inhabitants of the island began to exhibit disordered eating.

Television shows continue to feature impossibly thin actors in lead roles. More recently, reality shows such as *The Swan* and *Dr. 90210,* which feature plastic surgery and major makeovers, have been criticized for promoting unhealthy body image. In *The Swan* young women are separated from family and friends for several weeks to undergo an intensive diet and exercise plan. Hair stylists recommend hair extensions and highlights, and plastic surgeons perform breast augmentation, facelifts, and Botox [a paralytic neurotoxin that reduces facial wrinkles] and collagen injections. The . . . results are showcased in a beauty pageant, where formerly "ugly ducklings" compete against each other for the title of *The Swan.*

According to a recent study, children exposed to excessive TV viewing, magazines, and movies are at higher risk of obesity. When other variables are controlled, TV exposure independently increases the odds of becoming overweight by 50% for both men and women. Furthermore, the type of exposure, not the amount, is correlated with negative body image. Specifically, rates of exposure to soap operas, movies, and music videos were associated with higher rates of body dissatisfaction and drive for thinness. Excessive media consumption also may be correlated with the rate of childhood depression. This could be a function of negative body image, or may reflect the tendency of depressed kids to spend more time in front of the TV because of diminished energy.

As highlighted in a recent *Newsweek* article, classic eating disorders such as anorexia and bulimia are being diagnosed at younger ages (some as young as 8 or 9), and with higher frequency. A 1994 survey found that 40% of 9-year-olds have been on a diet. Clinicians now believe that eating disorders, previously ascribed to dysfunctional family dynamics, are multifactorial [dependent on various influences] in origin. [Although] family dynamics are certainly important, so too are biological predisposition to anxiety and mood disorders, interpersonal effectiveness skills, and cultural expectations of beauty. The development of pro-anorexia (pro-ana) and probulimia (pro-mia) websites on the Internet has been particularly concerning. Here, people who have made a "life style choice" to engage in eating-disordered behavior post messages detailing their weight loss progress and provide tips, support, and encouragement for their peers. Pictures of emaciated women resembling concentration camp victims serve as "thinspiration."

Men Are at Risk

Although fewer men meet criteria for anorexia and bulimia than do women, more men are becoming concerned with shape and weight. While some of the manifestations are similar to the disordered eating found in women, there are some important differences as well. Men too are bombarded by media pressure. Pictures of thin, muscular, and perfectly coiffed "metrosexual" models appear in men's magazines. Gay and straight men alike are shelling out significant sums of money for gym memberships, styling products, salon haircuts, manicures, and waxing treatments. [Shanna] Duggan and [David] McCreary found that reading muscle and fitness magazines correlated with levels of body dissatisfaction in both gay and straight men. Unlike Barbie, whose shape has become more realistic in recent years, action figures [doll toys marketed to males] have become increasingly muscular and devoid of body fat. In the "Adonis Complex," a phenomenon with similarities to body dysmorphic disorder and anorexia nervosa, young men become obsessed with bulk and muscle mass, which can lead to overexercise, dietary restriction, and abuse of anabolic steroids.

With media pressure to be thin and a multibillion dollar dieting industry at our disposal, higher rates of eating disorders in the population seem concerning, but [they] are also understandable. [Although] cultural standards of beauty are certainly not new, today's media is far more ubiquitous and powerful. However, the reasons behind the growing obesity epidemic are not entirely clear.

For the most part, members of society strive to lead healthy lives. In addition to preaching the cosmetic appeal of weight loss, news reports warn of the risks of obesity, including heart disease and stroke. Frightened and inspired, overweight individuals begin strict diet and exercise regimens. They may even lose weight. However, our society is unique in that there is a surplus of cheap, micronutrient-dense food available, which is being advertised by the same media outlets advertising thinness and warning of the risks of obesity. After restricting too heavily, dieters often feel deprived. They binge on the unhealthy foods seen in advertisements, gain weight, feel poorly about themselves, and perpetuate the cycle. [Fewer] than 5% of individuals who have lost 20 pounds are able to keep it off for 5 years. In short, dieters pin all of their hopes on overly restrictive diets that were doomed to fail from the start. This, combined with a relatively sedentary life style, is likely responsible for increasing rates of obesity and disordered-eating behavior, such as dietary restriction, binge-ing, and purging.

Baby Steps Toward Change

Clearly, the problem is complicated, and there are no easy so-lutions. Parents and health care providers alike have a respon-sibility to talk with children about media messages and healthy life styles. Parents can limit exposure to television and talk with children about the messages portrayed on TV shows and in advertising. The American Academy of Pediatrics' current guidelines suggest that children watch no more than 1 to 2 hours of quality television per day and that parents watch programs with their children so they can discuss the content together.

Advertising executives are paid hefty salaries to try to find a way into the consumer's psyche.

A strong cultural identity is thought to be protective against eating disorders, and families can use this to their ad-vantage by teaching children about the history of their ethnic or religious group. Furthermore, families can eat dinner to-gether on a daily basis. In addition to ensuring that all family members are getting a nutritionally balanced dinner, parents have the opportunity to inquire about children's experiences at school, and the family can brainstorm together when prob-lems arise.

In addition to providing regular family meals, parents need to take responsibility for providing healthy meals and snacks spaced at regular intervals throughout the day. They also need to allow for a reasonable number of treats so that kids do not feel deprived. Clinical experience consistently shows that individuals overeat when they are hungry or emotionally stressed; skipping meals during the day can lead to overeating at night. Moreover, studies have shown that children's eating behavior is influenced by the habits modeled by their parents and that parental concern about a child's weight can negatively affect a child's self-evaluation. Families can plan fun outdoor activities, which increase physical activity without subjecting children to shame about their physical shortcomings. Studies consistently have shown that life style changes are most effective when undertaken by the entire family.

Teaching Healthy Habits

Health care providers should be quick to address concerns about obesity but must be careful to adopt an empathic, non-shaming approach. It is important not to restrict what children eat, but to encourage a healthy amount of physical activity and a moderate, healthy diet. Parents and clinicians should discourage dieting, as it rarely works in the long term. In addition, they should try not to focus too much on appearance or weight, as perceived pressure to be thin can lead to disordered eating. Most importantly, parents, teachers, and members of the health care community can encourage children to develop strengths such as music, art, or sports to foster healthy self-esteem. It is important for children to focus on mastery of an activity rather than comparing themselves to others. When adults suspect mood disorders or eating problems, children should be referred promptly for diagnosis and treatment.

Finally, the government needs to allocate funds to produce exciting, media-driven advertising campaigns to provide information to kids and families about good nutrition, exercise, and healthy self-esteem. Messages need to be visible at school, on TV, and online. Media is a formidable opponent precisely because advertising firms have the financial resources to produce clever advertisements that convince consumers to buy their products. Advertising executives are paid hefty salaries to try to find a way into the consumer's psyche. Magazine editors need to find ways to incorporate images of average-sized adults and teenagers into their publications. In addition, they need to find ways to resist publishing advertisements featuring emaciated models.

Adults need to take responsibility for teaching children healthy habits, and one of the best ways to do so is by modeling healthy eating and exercise. However, the process will likely be a slow one, and we will need to be patient. As any parent can tell you, it is nearly impossible to get a child to agree to have an apple for a snack when they've just seen a compelling ad for the newest flavor of potato chips. Perhaps if children got consistent healthy messages from "cool" media sources at school, online, on TV, and at home, the messages would be more effective. The media is a formidable force, and one that is not going to change easily. However, it is not the only culprit; parental behaviors and family values play an important role in shaping children's development. The onus is on adults to find a way to harness media power for good instead of evil.

2

The Fashion Industry Glamorizes Anorexia

Booth Moore

Booth Moore is a fashion critic for the Los Angeles Times.

Amid spreading concern about fashion models' much-publicized bouts with anorexia, Europe has taken a tougher stance on models' weight and body mass index, yet the American fashion industry seems reluctant to act on calls for establishing self-imposed standards. Even though magazines' and designers' profits would not suffer from showing less-starved models, the women on American runways are still dangerously skinny.

There was the model, at the Oscar de la Renta show, in a fur vest, spindly arms sticking out like brittle twigs. And the one at Yeohlee who wasn't big enough to fill out her high-waisted skinny pants.

Alarmingly thin models may be the subject fashion can't stop talking about. But as shows here [New York] are proving: So far, talk is all the American fashion industry is willing to do.

A Call to Action

The Council of Fashion Designers of America [CFDA] issued recommendations six weeks ago [in late 2006] about health and weight but decided not to take steps to enforce them. . . . Instead [they] asked designers to police themselves. Tougher

Booth Moore, "Designers Still Use a Skeleton Crew," *Los Angeles Times*, February 7, 2007. Copyright © 2007, The Los Angeles Times. Reproduced by permission.

actions have already been taken in Spain, Italy and Brazil, where the death of a model from complications of anorexia in November [2006] set off a global weight debate. The American guidelines encourage education and a healthier working environment backstage but do not adopt a minimum body mass index [BMI], as officials did at Madrid Fashion Week.

The initiative (or lack of initiative) has been a heated topic of conversation at fashion week here, where the models don't seem to be getting any fleshier. The Chelsea Art Museum even has a new show, "Dangerous Beauty," that requires visitors to walk across a "tile" floor made from working bathroom scales to enter the exhibit. And on Monday [February 5, 2007], the CFDA held a panel discussion about the health of models, enlisting nutrition and fitness experts to defend its decision not to conduct weigh-ins.

Vogue magazine was out in full force, along with designers Tory Burch, Donna Karan, CFDA President Diane von Furstenberg and about 100 media and industry insiders. Of course, no one touched the yogurt, pastries or fruit served for breakfast. [People were] too busy trying to cover their bony behinds.

Determining Good Health

It's true, there is more that goes into determining health than a magic number (in Madrid, the minimum BMI is 18, or about 125 pounds for a 5-foot-10 model). Height, weight, activity level and genetics are also involved. But asking designers to make guesses, even educated ones, about who is at risk for having an eating disorder is ludicrous. The real question is why designers want to use models who are so thin that they can't tell if they are healthy or not. Don't they know jutting hip bones distract from the clothes?

You could blame Twiggy and lean-line 1960s fashion for bringing thin "in." Or 1990s heroin chic, when waifs Kate Moss and Stella Tennant were a trend switch from the Amazonian [physically substantial] models of the 1980s. Others whisper privately that gay men in the industry are to blame, for preferring women who look like boys.

What the industry wants is creative freedom without responsibility.

It's not difficult to see how you could develop an eating disorder if your career depended on it. At the forum, Natalia Vodianova, a 24-year-old Russian model who has appeared in advertising campaigns for Calvin Klein and Marc Jacobs, explained how industry pressure caused her weight to plunge to 106 pounds, when she began losing her hair. With the help of a doctor, she regained her health, only to hear designers complain about how her body had changed.

"I was lucky enough to be very much in demand, so I could ignore the criticisms," she said. "But if I had been weak, I hate to think what would have happened."

Waiting for Change

The problem isn't just designers. The pressure to be thin comes from all sides—editors, stylists, hairdressers, even boutique owners who refuse to stock sizes above 8. But for all the lip service the issue is getting, nobody seems ready to embrace real change.

Panelist Nian Fish, who has worked in public relations and runway show production at [media relations company] KCD for 30 years, said forcing designers to use bigger models would be like "asking Rubens [a baroque painter known for his ample female nudes] to paint skinny women or the New York City Ballet to use bigger dancers." So, what the industry wants is creative freedom without responsibility.

And what would really happen if designers cut their runway samples bigger and the models had to eat, not starve, to fit? *Vogue* would go on publishing, New York would continue to have fashion week, black would still be the new black and thin would still be in. Just not so thin.

3

Fashion Is Not to Blame for Anorexia

Naomi Hooke

Naomi Hooke is an anorexia survivor.

Despite popular belief that the fashion industry is responsible for many cases of anorexia among women, ultrathin models are not the main cause for girls trying to starve themselves. Often the reasons for denying oneself food are depression, anxiety, and the fear of being seen as a sexual human being. The impact fashion photographs have on dieting cannot be ignored, but anorexic models are symptoms of the disease, not the cause.

It was two days before Christmas, and for the third time in my 20-year-long existence I found myself having my blood pressure monitored, my blood taken for biochemical analysis and my mental state being assessed for risk of self-harm and suicide. Once again, I'd been admitted to an eating disorder unit, rescued from my own little world of self-destruction. The day before, I had filled my every hour with food (or rather the avoiding of it), exercise, my ongoing obsession with academic work and fantasies about a future where I wouldn't be there to spoil everything.

My parents came to visit, my younger sister excited in anticipation of present-opening. It hurt to sit up, and hurt to lie down, yet I refused to believe that this was due to starvation and muscle wastage. My family brought me a stocking, but I

Naomi Hooke, "Understanding Anorexia: A Thin Excuse," *The Independent*, September 18, 2007. Copyright © 2007 Independent Newspapers (UK) Ltd. Reproduced by permission.

couldn't understand how they would ever think I deserved nice things. I left the presents unopened for over a month.

A History of Hiding Food

I'd suffered from anorexia to varying degrees since I was 11, hiding food and concealing my body under layer upon layer of clothing, and once again it had caught up with me.

As London Fashion Week continues, the controversy surrounding "size zero" models is once again up for discussion. Prompted by the [2006] Madrid ban on models with a BMI [body mass index] below 18.5, fashion capitals around the world have undertaken enquiries into the links between eating disorders and the catwalk. Although any measure to protect models at risk of eating disorders is to be applauded, to believe that the fashion industry causes eating disorders is to completely misunderstand this most complex of illnesses.

At 11, I was showing early signs of puberty, and the prospect of an adult life ahead terrified me. I was afraid of responsibility, of a time when I would have to face the world without my parents' hands to hold. But most of all I was scared of men and sex.

Beauty has very little to do with eating disorders, and the desire to be thin is merely one of many symptoms.

Throughout my illness, even when I was motivated, I was convinced that recovery was impossible. But miracles do happen. I was in the grip of anorexia nervosa for more than eight years, but with a lot of help from family, friends and professionals, I was able to turn my life around.

Anorexia Is Not a Lifestyle Choice

Anorexia has often been perceived as a quest for model-like beauty, as a teenage fad or as a diet gone wrong. It has even been described as a lifestyle choice. Seldom is anorexia acknowledged as the life-threatening medical condition that it is. Many anorexics detest their bodies, refusing even to pose for family holiday snaps. I, like many of the eating disorder patients I have met, never sought beauty; instead, I spent years trying to make myself look as ill as possible in order to avoid male attention.

As far back as I can remember, my self-esteem was low and I lacked confidence. Children can be cruel, and although they weren't the "cause" of my eating problems, the bullying I endured throughout my school days only added to my feelings of self-hatred.

It is often assumed that the distress in anorexia revolves solely around food and weight. However, the vast majority of eating disorder patients have numerous other difficulties, including low self-esteem or confidence, lack of self-care, and social difficulties. Sufferers are often presumed to pore over the pages of glossy magazines and starve themselves in their aspiration to become glamorous, thinner-than-thin sex goddesses. From my own experiences and from those of numerous other eating-disorder patients I have met, I can say unequivocally that nothing could be further from the truth. Beauty has very little to do with eating disorders, and the desire to be thin is merely one of many symptoms. Rarely can a single "cause" be identified.

On the ward, Christmas had been and gone, and it was beginning to dawn on me that I would not be well enough to return to university. I was convinced that, once again, I had failed. During those weeks, I hit rock bottom. After years of pretending, I finally opened up to staff at the hospital, and began speaking about some of my troubling innermost thoughts.

Switching Sides

I had never felt so ill; the pain was excruciating. My memories of this hellish period are sketchy, but I have since been told that my kidneys were failing and that I was at risk of cardiac arrest. I had many meetings with the doctors, and eventually I agreed to be fed via nasal gastric tube. It was horrible when they passed the tube, though deep down I know it probably saved my life.

It was at this point that something flicked inside my head. It was as though I'd "swapped sides": I stopped fighting everyone who was trying to help me. As the weeks went on, my stomach ached as it was stretched to accommodate food again. It still took me hours to eat a bowl of soup, and I still had a tube up my nose, but nevertheless, things were getting better.

I wasn't an easy patient. I cried and screamed and threatened to run away. But in spite of everything, staff at the hospital never gave up on me, and I'll remain eternally grateful for every hug and kind word.

Although my first trip home was challenging, it did open my eyes. At last I began to see how much anorexia was holding me back. I was getting stronger, thinking more logically, and perhaps most importantly my sense of ambition was returning. I started to dream about getting back to university and one day being able to help people with mental illness myself.

I spent seven months as an in-patient and two more as a day patient. I regained a healthy body weight, spent numerous hours discussing my underlying fears and was slowly beginning to develop a sense of self-worth.

My fall into the dark world of anorexia was never influenced by fashion or waif-like celebrities, though I knew others whose recovery from life-threatening illness was indeed hindered by the Western world's culture of thinness. I believe that the British Fashion Council's guidelines will go some way to protect the models themselves (of whom 40 per cent are said to suffer from eating disorders). However, I see problems both with the approach taken in Madrid of banning models with a BMI under 18.5, and the recent health certification scheme proposed in Britain [In 2007, the British Fashion Council sought to require models to provide proof from specialists who treat eating disorders that an individual model is not unhealthily thin].

Weight Standards Are Not the Core

Although BMI can offer a crude measure of physical health, it can never quantify psychological distress. Despite popular belief, low weight is not the only danger of eating disorders. There have been times in my life in which my BMI has been in the healthy range and yet my eating behaviours and mental state were far from healthy. I would starve myself for days on end before my body gave in to the pains of hunger and I would binge, after which I would feel so disgusted with myself that I would make myself vomit and/or cut myself with razor blades.

As for doctors' certificates, it takes considerable time and skill to assess whether an individual has an eating disorder, not least because sufferers often go to great lengths to hide their illness. I've been there, told the lies and tricked the scales.

It is a fact that a higher proportion of models suffer from eating disorders than do the general population. The "grooming" and competitive atmosphere undoubtedly perpetuate eating disorders within the modelling profession, but I am personally of the opinion that young girls with existing eating disorders are selected by modelling agencies because of their tiny figures. But, although the fashion industry may be rife with anorexia, the majority of eating disorder patients have not become ill through catwalk influences. And nor are they models.

4

Internet Programs Can Help Fight Eating Disorders on College Campuses

National Institute of Mental Health

The National Institute of Mental Health (NIMH) was founded to research the roots, causes, and symptoms of mental illnesses to help prevent and cure them. NIMH funds research by scientists and supports more than 2,000 research grants and contracts at universities and other institutions across the country and overseas.

A large-scale study funded by NIMH has shown that an Internet-based intervention program can keep high-risk women from developing eating disorders. Even women who already show symptoms of anorexia or bulimia responded well to the program and showed a high success rate. Although more-definitive data is needed, the study indicates that inexpensive online programs might be an important tool for health care providers and schools to fight eating disorders.

A long-term, large-scale study has found that an Internet-based intervention program may prevent some high-risk, college-age women from developing an eating disorder. The study, funded by the National Institutes of Health's (NIH) National Institute of Mental Health (NIMH), was published in the August 2006 issue of the *Archives of General Psychiatry.*

The researchers conducted a randomized, controlled trial of 480 college-age women in the San Francisco Bay area and

"College Women at Risk for Eating Disorders May Benefit From Internet-based Intervention Program," National Institute of Mental Health, August 7, 2006. Reproduced by permission.

San Diego, Calif., who were identified in preliminary interviews as being at risk for developing an eating disorder. The trial included an eight-week, Internet-based, cognitive-behavioral intervention program called "Student Bodies," which had been shown to be effective in previous small-scale, short-term studies. The intervention aimed to reduce the participants' concerns about body weight and shape, enhance body image, promote healthy eating and weight maintenance, and increase knowledge about the risks associated with eating disorders.

The online program included reading and other assignments such as keeping an online body-image journal. Participants also took part in an online discussion group, moderated by clinical psychologists. Participants were interviewed immediately following the end of the online program, and annually for up to three years thereafter to determine their attitudes toward their weight and shape, and measure the onset of any eating disorders.

Anorexia generally is characterized by a resistance to maintaining a healthy body weight, an intense fear of gaining weight, and other extreme behaviors that result in severe weight loss.

New Technology May Help Patients

"Eating disorders are complex and particularly difficult to treat. In fact, they have one of the highest mortality rates among all mental disorders," said NIMH Director Thomas Insel, M.D. "This study shows that innovative intervention can work, and offers hope to those trying to overcome these illnesses."

Over the course of a lifetime, about 0.5 percent to 3.7 percent of girls and women will develop anorexia nervosa, and about 1.1 percent to 4.2 percent will develop bulimia nervosa.

About 0.5 percent of those with anorexia die each year as a result of their illness, making it one of the top psychiatric illnesses that lead to death.

Anorexia generally is characterized by a resistance to maintaining a healthy body weight, an intense fear of gaining weight, and other extreme behaviors that result in severe weight loss. People with anorexia see themselves as overweight even when they are dangerously thin. Bulimia generally is characterized by recurrent episodes of binge eating, followed by self-induced purging behaviors. People with bulimia often have normal weights, but like those with anorexia, they are intensely dissatisfied with their bodies. All eating disorders involve multiple biological, behavioral, and social factors that are not well understood.

The intervention appeared to be most successful among overweight women who had elevated body mass indexes (BMIs) of 25 or more at the start of the program. In fact, among these women in the intervention group, none developed an eating disorder after two years, while 11.9 percent of the women with comparable baseline BMIs in the control group did develop an eating disorder during the same time frame. BMI is a reliable indicator of a person's body fat by measuring his or her weight and height.

Encouraging Results

The program also appeared to help women in the San Francisco Bay area who had some symptoms of an eating disorder at the start of the program, such as self-induced vomiting; laxative, diet pill, or diuretic use; or excessive exercise. Of those in the intervention group with these characteristics, 14 percent developed an eating disorder within two years, while 30 percent of those with these characteristics in the control group developed an eating disorder during the same time frame.

The authors suggest that the intervention helped these high-risk women become less concerned about their weight and shape, while also helping them understand healthier eating and nutrition practices.

"This is the first study to show that eating disorders can be prevented among high-risk groups," said lead author C. Barr Taylor, M.D., of Stanford University. "The study also provides evidence that elevated weight and shape concerns are causal risk factors for developing an eating disorder," he added.

The study suggests that relatively inexpensive options such as Internet-based interventions can have lasting effects on women at high risk of developing an eating disorder. However, the authors note that the results cannot be generalized widely because there were differences in the women's baseline characteristics and treatment responses between the two sites used in the study.

Motivation Is Key

Also, the rate at which the women stuck with the program was very high—nearly 80 percent of the online program's Web pages were read—suggesting that the participants were unusually motivated. "Women who are less motivated may be less likely to participate in or stick with this type of long-term intervention," added Taylor.

In addition, women with restricted or no access to computers would not be able to benefit from an online intervention program. However, the authors conclude that such Internet-based programs may be a good first step in a diligent program designed to screen women for potential eating-disorder risks.

5

Internet Programs Fighting Anorexia Should Be Viewed with Skepticism

Page Rockwell

Page Rockwell is a project and content manager for Salon.com.

Online programs fighting anorexia in college-age women might contribute to students' health, but new Internet interventions should be viewed with skepticism. No matter their effectiveness among high-risk women, computers should not be an excuse for college administrators to cut down on counseling and access to health care staff.

Experts estimate that around 4 percent of girls and young women have anorexia and/or bulimia, with an additional 4 percent believed to struggle with subclinical eating disorders. (Eating disorders are 10 times more common in women than they are in men, though of course many men also struggle with eating disorders.) For those who suffer from these conditions, the consequences can be severe: Anorexia is deadlier than any other psychiatric illness—10 percent of those hospitalized for the condition will eventually die from it—and bulimia can cause lasting damage to sufferers' stomachs, esophagi and mouths. Both disorders can cause other complications like dehydration and cardiac problems, and may dangerously disrupt electrolyte levels. And, unfortunately, eating disorders are notoriously hard to cure.

Page Rockwell, "'Student Bodies', Student Selves," Salon.com, November 1, 2006. Copyright © 2006 Salon.com. This article first appeared in Salon.com, at http://www.salon.com. An online version remains in the Salon archives. Reprinted with permission.

For that reason, researchers are increasingly investigating preventive treatment options for those with known risk factors. Now, the *Washington Post* reports, an eight-week online program called "Student Bodies," pioneered by a research team at Stanford University, is having a positive impact on some test subjects.

For school administrators dealing with lots of students and tight budgets ... an easily disseminated prevention tool is downright "tantalizing."

Initially, this happy bulletin leaves me feeling a little skeptical. It is absolutely great news that experts are seeing results with low-cost, high-efficacy options for treating eating disorders. But peppily named programs like "Food, Mood and Attitude" and "Full of Ourselves" seem destined to be the butt of on-campus jokes. Plus, over the long term, Internet-based treatment options don't seem to offer much in the way of human supervision or accountability. University of Texas psychologist Eric Stice told the *Post*, "I can't think of a single computer-based eating disorders program that can hold a candle to these results"—but is that really saying much?

Well, maybe. A recent study put 480 female college students through the "Student Bodies" program and monitored them afterward, and though program participants generally didn't fare better than those in the control group, the program did seem to benefit young women in "two high-risk subgroups": those who had body-mass indices over 25 and those who exhibited dangerous behaviors like excessive exercise, laxative abuse or purging. Two years after participating in the program, none of the study subjects with body-mass indices over 25 had developed eating disorders, though 12 percent of their peers in the control group had. The *Post* further reports that, among those who "reported problem behaviors such as self-induced vomiting at the start of the study, 14 percent had developed an eating disorder at the two-year mark, compared with 30 percent of the control group."

Computers Cannot Replace Counselors

The researchers behind "Student Bodies" may make the program available to other schools and universities, and that's great news. For school administrators dealing with lots of students and tight budgets, Stice says the idea of an easily disseminated prevention tool is downright "tantalizing." Even considering the program's positive results, though, the prospect of administering the program to students who demonstrate risk factors but do not yet suffer from full-blown eating disorders seems daunting, especially since sufferers tend to be secretive about their symptoms. I hope university administrators don't come to view online programs as a replacement for in-person monitoring and counseling.

6

Insurance Companies Should Not Deny Treatment to Anorexics

Kathryne L. Westin

Kathryne L. Westin's daughter Anna died of anorexia at the age of 21, after the family's insurance company refused to pay for necessary treatment. In response, the Westins established the Anna Westin Foundation and the Anna Westin House, which provides personalized residential eating disorder treatment for adolescent and adult females.

Anna Westin suffered from anorexia nervosa and died at age 21. She was denied doctor-recommended treatment by her family's insurance company. The discriminatory policies of many insurers against diagnoses based on mental illnesses put patients' lives at risk. Only by passing necessary legislation will people with mental illnesses be adequately protected from arbitrary and harmful insurance industry standards.

It is an honor to be here today [March 27, 2007] to talk with you about the need for mental health parity [equal treatment] legislation. It is also a huge responsibility because I am speaking for the millions of Americans who are affected by mental illness and who have been denied treatment by their insurance companies. I am the voice for people who are vulnerable and suffering and who are desperate for your help. I probably understand this better than most because my daugh-

Kathryne L. Westin, "Testimony Before the Subcommittee on Health of the House Committee on Ways and Means," WaysAndMeans.house.gov, March 27, 2007. Reproduced by permission of the author.

ter Anna, who suffered from an eating disorder, was denied care when she needed it to save her life. I am here as a mother who paid the ultimate price for our country's unwillingness to pass parity legislation. My family's experience illustrates the suffering and unspeakable consequences when insurance companies are allowed to discriminate against people with mental illness. This discrimination is killing people and needs to stop now. Congressmen [Jim] Ramstad and [Patrick] Kennedy's parity bill, with comprehensive language that includes diagnoses like eating disorders, is a key step in saving lives.

Anorexia Is a Mental Illness

Before I talk about parity, I want to tell you about my daughter Anna. Anna was a spirited, vibrant, gifted young woman. She grew up in a small town in MN [Minnesota] with a family who cherished her. She had a smile that could melt your heart, and she was one of the kindest and most generous people I have ever known. She had dreams, goals, and a future full of promise and possibility until she was diagnosed with a deadly illness. Anna was diagnosed with a mental illness that affects over 10 million American women and 1 million American men, a disease that has the highest mortality rate of any psychiatric illness ... a death rate of up to 20 percent. Anna suffered from an eating disorder: anorexia. She died on February 17, 2000; she was just 21 years old.

Anna was first diagnosed with anorexia when she was 16 years old. I admit that my husband and I actually breathed a sigh of relief when she was finally diagnosed, because once we knew what illness she had we could get on with the treatment and healing. We had good insurance, and I was confident that she would get the care she needed. I really did believe the worst was over; I could not have imagined what was in our future.

Anna was treated in an outpatient setting when she was first diagnosed, and she seemed to fully recover. We were optimistic that she was back on track and that life would return to "normal." At the time nobody told me that recovery would most likely be gradual and could take years. We were totally blindsided when she relapsed and our insurance became the obstacle to her recovery.

I don't blame our insurance company for Anna's death— anorexia killed her—but I do hold them partially responsible.

When Anna relapsed in June of 1999, we knew that she was in for the fight of her life; she was extremely ill. Her symptoms included heart abnormalities, low blood pressure, kidney failure and dizziness, but we were confident that she would have access to the best care available. After all, our family had the best insurance money could buy, and we trusted that they would join us and be part of the "team" fighting to save her. We understood that by purchasing the "Cadillac" [most ample] of insurance plans, our family would be covered for both minor and major health problems. We never dreamed that insurance would be allowed to decide what illnesses are covered. I cannot even begin to describe our reaction when we learned that our insurance company had denied Anna the care her doctors told us was necessary. We had brought her to a hospital that specialized in treating eating disorders. She met criteria for a diagnosis of anorexia, and her doctors were recommending immediate inpatient care because she was in critical condition. Imagine our shock when we were told to take her home until the insurance company authorized her care. At first I thought it was a misunderstanding, but I soon realized that it was not a mistake. According to our insurance company, Anna's care was "not medically necessary." Suddenly we were forced to somehow "prove" that Anna was sick enough to get the care her doctors recommended. I could hardly believe that the medical director of the insurance company was given the authority to make decisions about her care without even examining her; decisions that would prove fatal. To this day I have trouble understanding how someone so sick could be treated so casually by insurance only because she happened to be diagnosed with a mental disorder.

Fighting the Insurance Company

I have no doubt that if I had brought Anna to the hospital that day with similar symptoms caused by a "physical" illness she would have been admitted without question and she would have gotten the best care available until she was fully recovered. Instead, Anna fought her eating disorder, and at a time when we should have been totally focused on helping Anna we were forced to put energy into fighting with our insurance company.

I don't blame our insurance company for Anna's death—anorexia killed her—but I do hold them partially responsible. Our insurance company repeatedly denied coverage for Anna's treatment, even though her treatment team (which included medical doctors, a psychiatrist, a psychologist, a dietician, and several other professionals) warned that intensive, specialized care was vital to save her life. Imagine an insurance company denying the necessary chemotherapy for a cancer patient. The insurance company's portrayal that treatment was not medically necessary encouraged Anna's own denial about the seriousness of her illness, a common trait of eating disorders. One of the most heartbreaking results of the denial was Anna's belief that, because we were paying for her care, she was a burden to our family and we would be better off if she were dead. The last words she wrote in her journal were: "My life is worthless right now. Saying goodbye to such an unfriendly place can't be as hard as believing in it. And, essentially my spirit has fled already."

Try to imagine what it would be like to watch your child struggle with a disease that ravages the body and the mind. To be a witness to the suffering, helplessness, and excruciating pain. I lived with Anna's hopelessness and despair, and I watched her gradually slip away from me. I was heartbroken watching her fight for her life, confronted with roadblocks all along the way that were constructed by people who made excuses like, "there is no effective treatment for eating disorders, so we don't pay for care." I knew that money and ignorance were the driving force behind the denials. I am confident that if this comprehensive mental health parity law had been in place, Anna's chances of survival would have been greater. She would not have felt like a burden, she would not have been stuck in the revolving door of treatment that only seemed to strengthen her illness, and she would have felt supported.

Discrimination Is Rampant

Sadly, it is too late for Anna, but it is not too late for the millions of Americans who suffer from eating disorders and other mental illnesses. The story you just heard is not unique; I talk to people every day who have similar experiences. I listen as parents cry and beg for help for their daughters and sons after insurance refuses to pay for care. I hear stories from families who have spent all of their savings, retirement, and college accounts and who have borrowed from family and friends and have no where else to turn. I know families who have taken out second and third mortgages on their homes to help cover the cost of care to save their child. It breaks my heart and makes me furious that we still have not passed parity and done all we can to insure that people get the care they need. It is an outrage that people who have purchased insurance and trust that they will be protected in the event of illness are still being denied care based on diagnosis. This IS discrimination!

After Anna died, I vowed to find a way to transform my grief and rage into something positive. Within days of Anna's death, our family founded the Anna Westin Foundation, and within months I joined the Eating Disorders Coalition for Research, Policy & Action, a Washington, D.C. based advocacy organization that has been working to increase awareness, educate policymakers, and promote understanding about the disabling and life-threatening effects of eating disorders. We have worked closely with Congressman Jim Ramstad and Congressman Pat Kennedy, and we are extremely grateful to them for their tireless efforts to pass mental health parity. We urge you to join them in support of this life-saving legislation. Every day we wait, another Anna dies unnecessarily of an eating disorder. We need a parity bill that includes eating disorders, substance abuse, and other mental illnesses. This bill will improve the lives of people with mental illnesses throughout the country, without preempting state laws that are already in place.

This is an exciting time; when I told my friends and colleagues that I was speaking to you today, it gave them much-needed HOPE. HOPE that the system can and will change, HOPE that their daughters and sons will finally have access to care, and HOPE that their voices will be heard. In 2001, immediately following the Help Panel's approval of Mental Health Parity, I spoke to my dear friend, the late Senator Paul Wellstone, and he told me how excited he was that parity was moving forward because it would finally end discrimination against people with mental illness. More recently, Congressman Jim Ramstad said: "It's time to finish what we started in 1994 with our good friend and colleague, the late Senator Paul Wellstone, and end discrimination against people with addiction. This is a life-or-death issue for millions of Americans." I agree with Congressman Ramstad; this is a life-or-death issue for millions of Americans. I urge you pass the "Paul Wellstone Mental Health and Addiction Equity Act" this session. I guarantee, it WILL save lives. Thank you.

7

Anorexia Might Be Related to Asperger Syndrome

Janet Treasure

Janet Treasure is an internationally renowned expert on eating disorders. She is a professor of psychiatry at King's College London and head of the Eating Disorders Unit at the South London and Maudsley National Health System Trust. She is the coauthor of Skills-based Learning for Caring for a Loved One with an Eating Disorder: The New Maudsley Method, *and also published* Anorexia Nervosa: A Survival Guide for Families, Friends, and Sufferers.

Research into the brain's neural networks suggests that anorexia might be related to Asperger's syndrome, a mild form of autism. Patients display the same cognitive inflexibility and often fail in looking at the larger picture, thus finding themselves overwhelmed by distracting details. These new findings do not invalidate the role society and culture play in contributing to eating disorders, however.

When I was training at the Maudsley [psychiatric hospital in London, U.K.] 30 years ago, anorexic girls were treated as little more than malfunctioning machines. Even when a friend at medical school became terribly thin and suddenly "disappeared" from class one day, no one talked about it.

Very little research had been done on eating disorders, and the causes remained a complete mystery to most psychiatrists.

Janet Treasure, "Is Anorexia the Female Asperger's?" *The Times* (London), August 17, 2007. Copyright © 2007 Times Newspapers Ltd. Reproduced by permission.

The view was that it was an illness that mainly affected middle-class, intelligent, white girls and was little more than an awkward phase of adolescence. Back then services were generally lacking, and treatments were borrowed from other areas of psychiatry and adapted to fit—a catch-all approach that spectacularly missed the incredibly complex causes of anorexia and bulimia.

Ten years later, while studying for my Medical Research Council fellowship, I became fascinated by the idea that brain mechanisms could contribute to a biological understanding of eating disorders. Twenty years on, there has been a huge change in the technologies available in understanding disease. The ability to decode the human genetic sequence means that, if a large enough sample of a particular disease is examined, and the DNA of those it affects is looked at, common risk factors emerge.

Traits that may appear present in childhood, such as obsessive-compulsive disorder or overperfectionism, can often indicate a vulnerability to developing an eating disorder later in adolescence.

Examining the Brain's Processes

What we now realise is that we need to be looking at underlying neural networks in the brain—how patterns of information are processed, how this affects both behaviour and the way an individual reacts to her environment, and why this goes wrong. We need to consider those aspects of how the brain functions that increase the risk of someone falling prey to an eating disorder.

I and others have been working hard to examine such processes and the research so far has produced very interesting findings that we have already been able to put into treatment programmes. We have found, for example, that people with eating disorders find it difficult to change self-set rules and learnt behaviour once fixed in the brain. They also see the world in close-up detail, as if they are looking at life through a zoom lens—but this can be at the cost of having an ability to see and think about self-identity and connections with others without getting lost in the details.

We also discovered that this distorted pattern of processing information has a strong similarity to autistic spectrums. It has even been described as the female form of Asperger's [an autism spectrum disorder]. Traits that may appear present in childhood, such as obsessive-compulsive disorder or over-perfectionism, can often indicate a vulnerability to developing an eating disorder later in adolescence.

Of particular interest are difficulties in "set shifting"—being able to shift back and forth between different tasks or mindsets. Problems may show up in a variety of forms: for example, cognitive inflexibility—an overrigid approach to problem-solving, and response inflexibility—excessively stereotyped behaviour. An example of this is an inability to deal with a last-minute change of plan, such as a meeting. Interestingly, we have found poor set-shifting ability even after recovery, and have found it in the healthy siblings of patients with anorexia.

Cognitive Inflexibility

This trait among healthy sisters implies set shifting or cognitive inflexibility could be an underlying aspect of eating disorders and therefore a possible target for treatment.

As well as poor set shifting, people with anorexia can show weak central coherence, which can be defined as a bias towards the local processing of information rather than placing it into a broader context. For example, if they were in a meeting, they would be distracted by somebody's fingernail and be unable to switch back to the matter in hand. This is one of the core features in cognition in autism spectrum disorders.

This trait became of great interest in eating disorders after a study a few years ago found the same kind of weak central coherence in people with anorexia as those with autism and Asperger's. The study also found that more than 20 per cent of the anorexic group could be described as having a disorder from within the autism spectrum.

So how can this translate into therapy? The new Maudsley model of individual treatment includes interventions focused on traits such as perfectionism and rigidity. With this new genetic-based research, it is helpful for us to know whether the markers we determine of underlying brain function run in families—and how much the external environment moderates them.

It is clear that exposure to media images depicting thin women really does reduce body-related self-esteem.

Examining other family members is very important, especially when there is another young woman in the family. The children of women who themselves have had an eating disorder are particularly interesting in this new area of research, as comparing patterns of the illness across generations can enhance our understanding of environmental as well as genetic factors and how they interact.

But it's not just about girls. Boys and young men seem to be more protected, perhaps by cultural factors in our society. But looking at the underlying brain function in male cases of eating disorders can improve our overall understanding. The risk factors, though rarer, tend to be more clearly defined.

Work on brain function, of course, does not exclude social and cultural triggers for eating disorders, the kind of thing that generates headlines about size zero models. It is clear that exposure to media images depicting thin women really does reduce body-related self-esteem. And the young models used to promote such images themselves may be at an increased risk of developing eating problems. But much of it happens in the home or playground, far from anything to do with fashion. Teasing and bullying focused on food and weight and body shape, particularly from family members, increases the risk of developing an eating disorder.

Eating disorders still have the highest mortality rate of any psychiatric illness. But there is a trend towards the numbers declining. I personally think a more optimistic outcome is within our grasp as we understand more and more the way the brain works.

8

Genes Cannot Explain Anorexia

Trisha Gura

Trisha Gura is a science journalist and medical writer. She is the author of the book Lying in Weight: The Hidden Epidemic of Eating Disorders in Adult Women.

Although researchers have found similarities between anorexia nervosa and Asperger syndrome, these commonalities don't constitute scientific proof of a link between the conditions. Nature might play a larger role in the development of anorexia than previously thought, but social environment determines who gets ill and who can avoid eating disorders.

They do it because their brains are wired to.

Girls with anorexia nervosa starve due to neural processing problems—much like those associated with Asperger's disorder, a mild form of autism.

That's the latest theory of eating disorders, proffered in *The Times* (U.K.) by Janet Treasure, head of the Eating Disorders Unit at the South London and Maudsley Hospital NHS Trust. In essence, faulty circuitry in the brain causes the restrictive, repetitive, and obsessive behaviors of both disorders. Those with anorexia target the abnormal patterning toward food. Those with Asperger's focus intensely on other areas of interest.

Trisha Gura, "Anorexia: Wired Like Asperger's?" WeighingIn-Blog.TrishaGura.com, August 24, 2007. Reproduced by permission of the author.

Parallels Between Asperger's and Anorexia

Treasure's controversial thesis is based, in part, on commonalities that the two disorders share.

According to eating disorder experts, individuals with anorexia generally express trademark personality styles through food:

- Perfectionism. *I want to look exactly like the fashion model ideal.*

- Anxiety. *I am terrified of being fat.*

- Extreme rule-making. *I will not eat more than 850 calories per day.*

- Preoccupation with and rigid adherence to those rules—to the point of social isolation. *I plan all my meals two days in advance and count out my calories religiously so as to never go over my quota. I cannot eat out with others.*

Experts say that individuals with Asperger's, too, have signature personality traits:

- Perfectionism (about areas of interest). *I know my teacher is wrong about Route 41 crossing Highway 91 at Main Street, because I memorized the street map of my town.*

- Hypersensitivity. *The world outside my mind overwhelms me.*

- Repetitive behaviors and rituals. *I go to the library every day to read about cartography.*

- Preoccupation and social isolation. *My love of maps seems at odds with the rest of the world. I live in a parallel universe.*

But while compelling, the observable similarities do not constitute scientific proof. "Just because it looks like a duck doesn't make anorexia an Asperger's duck," says clinical psychologist Richard Pomerance, PhD, who has seen a number of Asperger's patients in his private practice near Boston. He points out that there are at least as many symptoms of Asperger's—difficulty interpreting facial expressions and other social cues, for example—that do not show up in most anorexics.

Focusing on Neurobiology

Controversy aside, Treasure's theory certainly casts eating disorders in a new light. She says that anorexia is a disease grounded in human genetics and neurobiology. Genes orchestrate behaviors by coding for neurochemicals that signal each other in the brain, sometimes in abnormal ways.

This line of thinking is catching on within the eating disorders community. Researchers are using tools like DNA sequencers and PET [positron emission tomography] scanners to "look under the hood" at the brainwork behind self-starvation behaviors.

Molecular biologists are hunting down the genes for anorexia that might seed the mind with a predisposition for anorexia.

"Genes load the gun. Environment pulls the trigger."

The strongest candidates include genes involved with the serotonin system (which controls mood); dopamine centers (related to food repulsion, hyperactivity, and obsessive compulsive behaviors); and opioid receptors (involved in reward and feeding control).

Other researchers are scanning the brains of individuals with anorexia for clues to the processing centers that might go awry. Again, serotonin pathways top the list.

Even evolutionary biologists are stepping up to the plate and offering their own hypotheses as to why anorexia lingers in the human species. At first blush, anorexics should be out of the game, given that infertility is a common effect of the disease. The answer may be that those who can exist on minimal calories during times of scarcity can keep the tribe alive and, in doing so, pass the culprit genes on to the next generation. It's survival of the species rather than the individual that matters.

Culture and Environment Are Important Factors

But these biological underpinnings are only part of anorexia's complex mechanics, and Treasure is careful not to dismiss studies that point to culture and psychological issues as causes of and catalysts for eating disorders. Those studies do abound. For example, there is Anne Becker's work showing that the introduction of television into a population of Fijian teenage girls caused a surge of eating disorders in just three years. And numerous studies show that sexual abuse, trauma, and even bullying can catalyze eating disorders.

So it seems that anorexia nervosa is rooted in both nature *and* nurture. From the nature and nurture perspective, a person may be born with "bad" genes, which produce faulty neurotransmitters and/or circuits. An individual with such a genetic make-up is a time bomb for distorted thinking about body image. Then, something in the person's environment eventually may light the fuse.

This makes sense when I hear stories like those of Laura, 65. . . . She was diagnosed with anorexia as a teen, recovered by 20, relapsed at 48, then recovered again. Laura is an identical twin. Her sister never had anorexia, and is, in fact, obese.

How do we explain the phenomenon of Laura and her sister, where two women share exactly the same genes but only one gets anorexia? Same genetic makeup, different life experiences.

As psychologist Cynthia Bulik, PhD at the University of North Carolina, Chapel Hill, sums it up, "Genes load the gun. Environment pulls the trigger."

9

Anorexia Is More than a Genetic Predisposition

Kate Taylor

Kate Taylor is a culture reporter at The New York Sun *and the editor of* Going Hungry: Writers on Desire, Self-Denial, and Overcoming Anorexia.

From endocrinology to feminist research, society has never lacked theories to try to explain why people suffer from anorexia nervosa. Yet each new theory has been as reductionist as the last, and the causes of anorexia still elude scientists and social theorists. A new theory that genetics is responsible for anorexia neglects the fact that anorexia has been on the rise ever since the turn of the twentieth century and, like its predecessors, paints anorexics as victims of their illness. Yet anorexia also contains an element of choice, and until scientists examine what makes the illness desirable to its victims, they will fail to fully grasp this complex phenomenon.

Last month [November 2005], *Newsweek* tried to put a new face on anorexia. No, not the doe-eyed brunette on the magazine's cover, but the article inside trumpeting the latest theory about the disease: It's genetic. According to *Newsweek*, the appearance of anorexia among groups not conventionally associated with it (younger girls, nonwhite girls, boys) has made doctors reject the old idea that victims "catch" the disease from cultural influences or pressure-cooker families. Now,

Kate Taylor, "Is Anorexia Genetic? What the Newest Theory Leaves Out," Slate.com, December 19, 2005. © Copyright 2005 Washington Post. Newsweek Interactive Co. LLC. Reproduced by permission.

doctors compare anorexia to autism and schizophrenia—diseases that psychologists once blamed on parents and that science later showed to be hardwired.

Genetic determinism is the latest in a long line of reductive theories of anorexia. Since the start of the 20th century, the disease has been seen through the prisms of endocrinology, Freudian psychoanalytic theory, developmental psychology, and feminist cultural criticism. It's easy to see why these theories became prevalent. Each offers a simple explanation for anorexics' behavior—brain chemistry, sexual anxiety, a controlling mother, fashion magazines—and in doing so, demystifies a maddeningly opaque disease. And because anorexia is so complex, each theory gets at least part of it right. But the most appealing thing about these interpretations is that they sidestep one particularly disturbing aspect of anorexia, which is that it's at least partly voluntary and willful. That a 10-year-old would choose to do something so counter to nature is hard to accept, so these interpretations of anorexia make her its unwitting victim. Genetic determinism takes such thinking to a logical extreme: It's not her fault; it's in her genes.

From the time the diagnosis was first conceived, experts have discounted anorexics' motives. The disease was named in 1873 by doctors who likened anorexia—a new phenomenon of young girls starving themselves—to hysteria: Both afflictions were thought to result from dangerous upheavals in the bodies of maturing girls. Few 19th-century doctors devoted much thought to anorexics' rationales for their self-starvation. If a girl said she couldn't eat, and offered some excuse like a stomachache, her claim was taken at face value; such symptoms were assumed to be psychosomatic, just like a hysteric's fits of weakness or paralysis. Only one doctor—the "father of hysteria," neurologist Jean-Martin Charcot—suggested that anorexics were motivated by a conscious desire to be thin.

At the beginning of the 20th century, doctors began to seek physiological explanations for anorexia. The hot new field was organotherapy, and early endocrinologists were busy injecting patients with "organ juices" in order to remedy various defects. After the discovery in 1913 of an emaciated woman who had died and turned out, on autopsy, to have a shrunken pituitary gland, doctors began to inject pituitary extract into anorexics. In the '20s, physicians at the Mayo Clinic briefly treated anorexia as a metabolic disorder and tried injecting anorexics with thyroid hormone. Others gave them insulin or estrogen. But the treatments were unsuccessful: The only anorexics who gained weight on hormones were simultaneously being fed a rich diet. By 1940, the idea that anorexia was an endocrine disease had been rejected.

By the '90s, health-class presentations on eating disorders often involved rifling through magazines and discussing how unreasonably skinny the models were.

The rise of psychoanalysis around this time led doctors to focus on the psychological causes of the disease. In a 1939 study, a psychoanalyst named George H. Alexander found that one girl's dieting began after two classmates had become pregnant and left school, and deduced that she'd developed a paranoid fear of pregnancy. Based on this single case, Alexander concluded that anorexia was caused by a belief that fat is pregnancy and food an impregnating agent. For a while, this view was taken seriously; into the '60s, doctors referred anorexics to analysts who subscribed to it. But soon, more complex and credible psychological theories emerged.

These theories, developed in the 1960s and '70s by people like Hilde Bruch in the United States and Mara Selvini Palazzoli in Italy, were more empirical and sensitive than most of those that preceded—or followed. Bruch and Palazzoli explained anorexia in developmental and cultural terms. *Newsweek*'s gloss of Bruch's 1978 book, *The Golden Cage*—"that narcissistic, cold and unloving parents (or, alternatively, hypercritical, overambitious and overinvolved ones) actually *caused* the disease by discouraging their children's natural maturation to adulthood"—doesn't do her ideas justice. Both Bruch and Palazzoli did, as *Newsweek* says, attribute anorexia partly to a girl's failure to develop a sense of independence, but they didn't blame that exclusively on parents. They also linked anorexia to the increasing glamorization of thinness and popularity of diets. The cultural endorsement of thinness, in their view, merely set the conditions that allowed particular girls to discover, in manipulating their appetites and their bodies, sensations of power and accomplishment that they otherwise lacked.

The disease often makes them feel special and unique.

Bruch's description of the tensions in anorexics' families caught the public's attention. Then, in the late '70s and early '80s, popular feminist writers took up the cause. Books like Susie Orbach's *Fat Is a Feminist Issue*, Kim Chernin's *The Obsession: Reflections on the Tyranny of Slenderness*, and, 10 years later, Naomi Wolf's *The Beauty Myth* attributed anorexia to a misogynistic culture that glorified waifs and denigrated real women. By the '90s, health-class presentations on eating disorders often involved rifling through magazines and discussing how unreasonably skinny the models were. Even when I was 12, this struck me as reductive: What girl would possibly be moved to such extremes by an ad for a depilatory?

The new genetic theory, like the others, seems partly right and partly wrong. After all, genetics can't explain why anorexia proliferated in the late 20th century, any more than a narrow feminist argument explains why, even though we're all confronted with images of [supermodel Gisele Bundchen's] improbable physique, only some people become anorexic. An appropriately complex theory of anorexia would address both environmental and individual factors, in order to explain why it became widespread in the last 40 years and why, still, only certain people get it.

Interestingly, the most incisive interpretations of anorexia often fail to stick in the public consciousness. Two doctors who treated anorexics in Toronto in the 1930s left behind a remarkably astute description of the type: "Most of them are intelligent, some to a marked degree; all are highly sensitive," they wrote. "Usually they are impulsive, willful, introspective, and emotionally unstable." Then, refuting the cliché that anorexics are ruled by insecurity, the doctors suggested instead that they're driven by positive desires: "They have a strong desire for prominence and dominance."

From my own experience (I first had the disease when I was 10) and those of other people I've talked to, this last observation is one of the most important—and least acknowledged. It's easier to see anorexics as victims, whether of social forces or biology, than to imagine that they derive pleasant sensations from their behavior. But they do. The disease often makes them feel special and unique. Until we discard the victim model and admit that anorexia, though destructive, often fulfills a deep personal need, we can't begin to investigate what makes a person vulnerable to it. Evidence that anorexia now affects an unexpectedly wide range of people provides an impetus for a new, more complex theory of the illness. But any such theory must acknowledge the willful aspect of anorexia, instead of trying to turn the disease into something as random and involuntary as a cold.

10

Pro-Anorexia Web Sites Put Young People at Danger

Constance Rhodes

Constance Rhodes is the founder and president of FINDING-balance, a Christian health and wellness organization with an emphasis on eating disorders. She's the author of Life Inside the "Thin" Cage: A Personal Look into the Hidden World of the Chronic Dieter *and* The Art of Being: Reflections on the Beauty and the Risk of Embracing Who We Are.

Pro-anorexia Web sites pretend to offer support to anorexics, but instead prey on the victims of the disease. They feast on almost pornographic pictures of extremely thin women and portray underweight bodies as ideal. On so-called pro-ana Web sites, eating disorders are treated like a religion, and Christian psalms are reappropriated to propagate cruel and unhealthy rules. Caregivers should be aware of these sites, fight the messages they contain, and offer help to individuals suffering from eating disorders.

Sixteen years ago [in 1991] I was a freshman at Bible College, dabbling for the first time in the dangerous territory of disordered eating, as I desperately tried to lose the 15 pounds I had gained during my first few months away from home. For the next decade, I would struggle with anorexia, bulimia, binge eating and a long pattern of chronic dieting that kept me trapped in a cage of insecurity, obsession and isolation. Looking back now, I can't even imagine how my al-

Constance Rhodes, "Pro-Anorexia Websites," CPYU-Center for Parents and Youth Understanding, www.cpyu.org. August 23, 2007. All content © 2007, Group, Inc. Reproduced by permission.

ready self-destructive behavior would have intensified had I had access to something unheard of at the time: pro-anorexia Web sites.

If you are someone who works with young people today, particularly young girls, it's vital to understand the phenomenon of Web sites that actively promote disordered eating. Such sites are often referred to as pro-ana (anorexia) and/or pro-mia (bulimia). For the purposes of this article, however, we'll simply refer to them as pro-ed (eating disorders). . . .

Tone and Feel

In general, the bulk of the sites' content is written by bright, studious and creative girls who are themselves struggling with eating disorders. The tone varies from somewhat immature views and writing styles to those that are deeply philosophical and brilliantly conveyed, however unhealthy their message.

On a positive note, creative expression is often promoted through the sharing of poetry, song lyrics and stories written by those familiar with the struggle. Unfortunately, however, there is also no shortage of foul, angry and frustrated language, sometimes communicated by the site host, and more often by those who write in to share their opinions.

Another fairly consistent aspect of pro-ed sites is the portrayal of women as sexual objects.

When it comes to the feel of these sites, most of those I visited were very dark visually, often featuring a black or dark background with reversed out text which is usually white but sometimes red or other colors that may not be easy to read. This unappealing design style probably stems from the fact that many young site hosts have little experience designing Web sites, and/or may simply be mimicking other sites. But I also feel it is a reflection of the inherent darkness of this disease (or "lifestyle," as pro-ed sites prefer to call it). I did find one or two sites featuring clean, light colored pages with tastefully arranged text, but these seem to be the exception, not the rule.

Sexual Objectification of Women

Another fairly consistent aspect of pro-ed sites is the portrayal of women as sexual objects. Depending on the personal taste (and sometimes weight) of the site host, these images can vary, from beautiful, normal-bodied women, to slim celebrities, to shockingly skeletal anorexics (think Karen Carpenter [American singer who died in 1983 of heart failure, due to anorexia nervosa], minus 15 or 20 pounds).

And then there are the images I would consider to be of a more pornographic nature. For example, a site titled "Fragile Innocence" opens with an image of a woman—completely nude with the exception of a pair of shin-length black boots—lying on her side on a dirty floor. Her bent arm covers her face and the photo has been artistically altered to incorporate red, orange and yellow tones, adding darkness and increasing the tension of the image. The caption reads "wasted."

While not all sites feature imagery of this dark a nature, many include photos of women wearing a vacant, hollow stare. And many of them are nude or scantily clad.

"It's not surprising that these sites feature highly sexual content," says Ann Capper, a nutritionist who works with disordered eaters. "Girls and women are consistently objectified and sexualized in the media. The site hosts are only mimicking what they see."

Dr. Carla Garber, a Texas psychologist with more than 20 years' experience treating eating disorders takes it a step further. "Often those afflicted with EDs are confused about sexuality, and many have experienced sexual abuse," she says. "Unfortunately, the body degrading and pornographic aspects of these sites serve to further the individual's disconnection and hatred of his/her body."

But actual site hosts don't always see things this way. "I think you should be aware of the line between nudity and pornography," writes Lisa, an 18-year-old pro-ed visitor and site host. "I don't see that ['Fragile Innocence'] picture as erotic; rather, the nudity is expressing the stripped-nakedness of what appears to be a breakdown."

And Katie, a 15-year-old who spends 52 hours a week on pro-ed sites (including her own) tells me, "There is really no relation between pornography and our 'thinspiration' pics . . . it's just saying 'look, this is how thin I am without my clothes on . . . you wanna be like this don't you?' Nothing really more."

In addition to photos of thin women, several sites also feature "reverse thinspiration" images of overweight or grossly obese women, designed to scare the visitor into "sticking with the program."

Regardless of what site hosts believe about the photos they post, it is clear the objectification of women is a large and unavoidable influence on these sites and in regard to eating disorders in general. It should also be noted that, while significantly fewer in number, there are sites aimed at males that objectify men in a similar manner.

"Thinspiration"

A prominent feature on any self-respecting pro-ed site, the "thinspiration" section can normally be split into two parts: images and quotes/writings designed to help "inspire" the visitor to continue further on into their disordered eating behavior.

Images can range from photos of normal-bodied, pretty women to those who are nearly dead of self-starvation. Many of the sites feature the same gaggle of celebrities (termed "idols" by some), including Kate Moss, Christina Aguilera, Calista Flockhart and Debra Messing. Some sites keep track of celebrities' weight fluctuations, showing "high weight" and "low weight" photos of selected stars. Others include "bone pictures"—shocking photos of anorexics in the final stages of the disease, with so little flesh that their bones and veins are painfully visible.

In addition to photos of thin women, several sites also feature "reverse thinspiration" images of overweight or grossly obese women, . . . designed to scare the visitor into "sticking with the program." Cartoons, drawings and other artistic expressions related to dieting, starving, exercising, etc. may also appear. Normally the images are accompanied by a thinspiration quote.

Very popular on these sites, thinspiration quotes range from the innocuous, "A moment on the lips, forever on the hips" and "You can never be too rich or too thin," to the more forceful, "If it tastes good, it's trying to kill you" and "Hunger hurts but starving works."

On many sites, stronger exhortations appear, such as this one: "You've made a decision: you will NOT stop. The pain is necessary, especially the pain of hunger. It reassures you that you are strong, can withstand anything."

Distractions

Another popular feature is lists of "distractions"—things to help keep a person's mind off the fact they are starving. Some of these I found were, "go on a walk," "clean your house until everything looks untouched," and "read the newspaper—every word of it."

The sites readily acknowledge that everything in life must now revolve around eating, calories and weight, and are full of ideas about how to stay "on track" with one's eating disorder.

Offering a glimpse of the struggle are so-called creeds, codes and "psalms" that reveal the ideology of the disordered eater's world. Following are two examples from a site called "Fragile Innocence":

Ana's creed

I believe in CONTROL, the only force mighty enough to bring order to the chaos that is my world.

I believe that I am the most vile, worthless and useless person to ever have existed on the planet, and that I am totally unworthy of anyone's time and attention.

I believe that other people who tell me differently are idiots. If they could see how I really am, then they would hate me almost as much as I do.

I believe in PERFECTION and strive to attain it.

I believe in salvation through trying just a bit harder than I did yesterday.

I believe in bathroom scales as an indicator of my daily successes and failures.

I believe in hell, because I sometimes think that I am living it.

I believe in a wholly black and white world, the losing of weight, recrimination for sins, abnegation of the body and a life ever fasting.

Psalm

Strict is my diet. I must not want. It maketh me to lie down at night hungry. It leadeth me past the confectioners. It trieth my willpower. It leadeth me into the paths of alteration for my figure's sake ... Before me is a table set with green beans and lettuce. I filleth my stomach with liquids. My day's quota runneth over. Surely calorie and weight charts will follow me all the days of my life, and I will dwell in the fear of scales forever.

The fact is, there is a very powerful enemy living and breathing at these sites. He is present in the images, the words and the design.

These writings reflect the often cult-like religious fervor with which many extreme disordered eaters approach their relationship with food. Notice the high level of self-hate conveyed—a key indicator of the incredible role that love can play in bringing a disordered eater to a healthier place. . . .

A Difficult Battle

If you've never experienced an eating disorder, you might be wondering, "Why would anyone willingly choose to 'obey' such a cruel master?" It's important to know that eating disorders, especially when they reach extreme stages of anorexia or bulimia, rob their victims of much more than healthy eating habits. A disordered eater does not have the balanced nutrition necessary for [her] brain to function well, and for [her] to make logical and healthy decisions. Indeed all parts of [her] being—physical, mental, emotional and spiritual—are compromised as [she falls] further into the disorder. For these and other reasons it can be difficult to help those who struggle with disordered eating, especially if you are not experienced in this area. . . .

Bottom Line

As a recovering disordered eater, I could write pages of commentary on what I found while researching pro-ed sites, but there simply isn't room to do so here. What I will say is this: even though these sites do provide a welcoming "community" for those seeking understanding of their issues, they do not offer peace, help or hope for healing. Instead, even the best-intended are still places of darkness, hopelessness and despair.

The fact is, there is a very powerful enemy living and breathing at these sites. He is present in the images, the words and the design. He is the one sparking the angry, frustrated and offensive writings posted on message boards and in chat rooms. And he is the one doling out enough rope [with which] to hang oneself to those who so desperately need something to cling to.

The Internet is not something we can avoid or ignore, and while several pro-ed sites have been successfully shut down, many more will continue to pop up in their place. With this in mind, we must take bold steps to help those who are lost find the love, support and help that they need. And to do this we must be aware of what kind of enemy we are fighting.

11

Pro-Anorexia Web Sites Need to Be Removed

Health E-Zine

Health E-Zine, part of the Lilith E-Zine, is a nonprofit online magazine focusing on health issues.

With the help of the Internet, anorexics worldwide promote their disease as a lifestyle, talk about the virtues of eating as little as possible, and provide tips to like-minded people on how to hide their condition from worried parents and doctors. Pro-anorexia Web sites are an expression of this complex mental illness that wants to both hide and draw attention to itself at the same time. The sites are especially dangerous to teenagers on the verge of becoming anorexic, who feel accepted by the online community and as part of an elite group. Teenagers and college students need to be protected from this dangerous influence, and pro-anorexia Web sites must be shut down.

Anorexics aren't just starving themselves to death, they are also starved for attention and live extremely lonely lives. It takes years of obsessive self-destructive behaviour to develop the eating disorder, and most people don't understand it or want anything to do with the person (unless it is to try and convince them to eat more).

A Suicidal Lifestyle

Over time anorexics lose friends, become incredibly depressed and lonely. Unfortunately the Internet is now connecting anorexics with one another, providing them with support and

Health E-Zine, "Anorexia on the Internet," Health.lilithezine.com, November 14, 2008. Reproduced by permission.

friendship for a "lifestyle" that can best be described as suicidal. Pro-ana groups, as they are now called, are groups of anorexic people who believe that anorexia is not [an] eating disorder but a choice of lifestyle.

After all, they did make the choice to starve themselves. It is arguably a lifestyle choice.

But as a lifestyle it is also harmful, because the groups promote, quite literally, starving yourself to death. Members brag about doctor visits, heart attacks, the severity of their symptoms and more. In their narrow tunnel vision they have only partially succeeded and won't be happy until they have truly starved themselves to death.

Anorexics and would-be anorexics around the globe can access more than 400 websites designed solely for them.

Starved themselves for the sake of what? Trying to look attractive? Trying to get attention? Fear of obesity? The same or similar arguments are made by obese patients who want attention, are afraid of being too thin. Obesity is another . . . eating disorder wherein cyclical depression causes them to eat more when sad, trying to reward themselves with food.

For anorexics it is the opposite: starving themselves as punishment.

Thanks to the wonders of the Internet, anorexics and would-be anorexics around the globe can access more than 400 websites designed solely for them. Need to know how to disguise your weight loss so concerned friends will stop hounding you to eat more? Looking for a few words of support as you launch into your latest deprivation diet? Or perhaps you would like to know the tricks for satisfying that pesky weekly weigh-in at the doctor's office? It's all right here.

They claim they don't want help, they claim they don't want attention, they claim just want to support each other and help other people to become anorexic like themselves.

Insights into Anorexia

The websites provide a fascinating insight into the world of anorexics and their obsession with starvation. For eating disorder educators, the very language of the sites can provide invaluable hints into a troubled psyche. "I think some of these sites are worded in a way that indicates the hosts do want help," says Vivian Meehan, president and founder of the National Association of Anorexia Nervosa and Associated Disorders, or ANAD. "They're putting themselves out there. But then they also put up a defense against it. Don't come on the site if you're only interested in putting us down."

That psychology plays out almost to the letter on one of the most visible pro-anorexia sites . . . known as "My Goddess Ana," as if anorexia was also a religion. Accused in the press of perpetuating a deadly disease, one site's 20-year-old creator offers this reply. "The opening page of the site clearly stipulates that the content of the site is Pro-Anorexic and should not be viewed by those who are in recovery or are thinking about recovery, or who, indeed, do not suffer from an ED [eating disorder]. If you are reading this as an objector to Pro-Ana sites, why did you enter in the first place when the entrance page has told you not to?"

Once you're inside the websites there are constant slogans designed to boost the reader's sense of self-starvation and mind set.

Which, in short, is utter bullshit. These girls and women (and rarely men) have been lying to themselves so long they would sooner prostitute themselves than admit they are just fooling themselves.

Sexual Content

And sometimes they do. Sex is a big theme on pro-ana websites, frequently with images of skantily clad women who have starved themselves to skin and bones. Apparently there is no shortage of men (with low self-esteems) willing to sleep with a skeleton.

The websites have straightforward warnings like:

"This is a PRO-ANOREXIC site. The information in the following pages contains pro-anorexic material. For this reason, it should NOT be viewed by anyone who is in recovery or who is considering recovery."

"Please, if you do not already have an eating disorder, turn back now. If you are in recovery, turn back now. Anorexia is a deadly disease. It is not to be taken lightly."

Which sounds like responsible advice, until you consider the effects of a warning like that on the psychology of anorexia. The sites' users, usually young women suffering from anorexia, tend to be perfectionists dead-set on gaining approval. It's a very tough mind set to maintain, and you can . . . do it [only] if you're willing to suffer (which anorexics are only too happy to do) and if you can be strong in the face of adversity (i.e., food and the people who are trying to get you to eat).

Once you're inside the websites there are constant slogans designed to boost the reader's sense of self-starvation and mind set. Slogans like: "Stay strong," "Thinspiration," and others.

In other words, if you're a young woman on the verge of anorexia, and you visit this site and read the warning, chances are you're going to see it as a dare. Think of anorexia as the negative marathon of eating disorders: If it were easy, everyone would do it, and then what kind of cachet would it have?

Once past the warning screen, visitors are exhorted to "Stay strong!" (in the face, one presumes, of parents, friends or doctors who are pushing food on them). It's a bizarre dichotomy of messages, and it forms the crux of this phenomenon. Yes, the websites seem to be saying, this site is dangerous, and it could be harmful to your health. On the one hand, we accept that we are sick, that we have an eating disorder and we are interested in spreading our illness, we are proud of our illness—and once you've joined our ranks, we'll do whatever it takes to enable your quest for the "perfect" body.

Looking for "Role Models"

This labored enthusiasm serves as a red flag to eating disorder educators like Meehan. "One of the primary goals of anorexics is to persuade others that they are perfectly fine, and that they have the right to lead their lives however they see fit," says Meehan. "And one of the ways of doing that is to find other people who are achieving those goals—so these websites provide not only reinforcement, along with a forum for exchanging and picking up tips."

It's not just about tips, however. Throughout the sites, visitors are bombarded by images of waif-thin fashion models and movie stars. Some have been altered to appear emaciated. Others are, perhaps even more disturbingly, left untouched. Either way, the effect is immediate: Revulsion followed by a kind of morbid fascination. How on earth did she get to be that thin? Then moving on to the barrage of "Thinsprirations," as one site names its pro-thin quotes. ("Nothing tastes as good as being thin feels," reads one.)

To date at least 115 pro-anorexia sites have been removed from Yahoo! servers.

The problem, of course, is that most of the minds visiting these sites are not exactly in peak psychological condition. And many of the sites, with their rosy color schemes and celebrity slide shows, are designed to appeal to the most vulnerable population: Recent studies indicate that 85 percent of anorexics experience the first onset of illness by age 20—and they're only getting younger. Researchers have noted a marked increase of cases in the 8[-year-old] to 11-year-old age range over the past 5 years.

Kids in that age range (perhaps not coincidentally) are also spending more and more time in front of computers, educators note, a trend that leaves them especially susceptible to the proliferation of pro-anorexia sites.

Until recently Yahoo! and Geocities (owned by Yahoo!) websites hosted by far the most pro-anorexia sites of any web portal. Googling "anorexia" produces mixed results: Some are pro-recovery, but many others promote the cycle of starvation.

In recent years, however, [Yahoo's] self-described commitment to the safety of adolescents and children has caused them to remove the pro-anorexia sites from its server: "The fact is that most people who become anorexic first experience symptoms before they are eighteen," says ANAD vice president Christopher Athas. "Yahoo! claims to be interested in the health and welfare of children? Here's a good chance to prove it."

To date at least 115 pro-anorexia sites have been removed from Yahoo! servers.

A company spokesperson explains that "Content with the sole purpose of creating harm or inciting hate is brought to our attention, we evaluate it, and in extreme cases, remove it, as that is a violation of our terms of service."

The Future of Pro-Ana Sites

Does this mean pro-ana websites will have their days numbered? I would argue yes. Even if they aren't removed by prudent businesses, the creators themselves will eventually starve themselves to death, and the websites will be removed or ignored as time goes on. Nothing on the Internet is permanent.

But it does mean that new generations of pro-ana websites will appear, and their messages need to be removed quickly.

12

"Pro-Ana" Is a Religion and Its Members Are Misjudged

ProThinspo.com

Prothinspo.com is a pro-anorexia Web site that promotes anorexia as a positive lifestyle choice.

Pro-ana (pro-anorexia) is a religion and should not be judged by others. It is not pro-death, nor does visiting a pro-ana site cause or encourage anorexia. Its followers use online forums for inspiration and support.

Is Pro-Ana your religion? Well, it seems that if it is your religion, people should not judge you based on it. Fellow Prothinspoers, I know how you feel when people judge you. I just wanted to say, believe what you want to believe and follow your dreams. On this planet, you can be whatever religion you want to be! I surfed the web and found some more info I thought you would like to read.

Myth: Pro-Ana Prays to Anorexia

Reality: There is reference to a religion of sorts that exists on Pro-Ana websites, with several referrals of the name "Ana" mentioned. But people, mainly the media and anti[-Ana people] get confused and spread the misinformation that Ana refers to anorexia. The name Ana in the religious connotation actually is [part of] the full name Anamadim, and not some goddess named anorexia. . . . Anamadim was the creation of a site by the name of Underground Grotto, where there is even

Prothinspo, "Pro-Ana Religion Talk," ProThinspo.com, 2008. Reproduced by permission.

a summoning spell to invoke Anamadim. However, there is an extremely slim (no pun intended) minority of those on Pro-Ana sites that partake in this religious-style activity. This also has nothing to do with the letters, creeds, commandments, etc. either. It has nothing to do with the huge majority of Pro-Ana.

Myth: The Entire Pro-Ana Religion [Was Created Online]

Reality: The Pro-Ana religion seen on many Pro-Ana sites was never created by any Pro-Ana site at all. All the creeds, letters, commandments are . . . made by professional psychologists in an attempt to make the mindset of the anorexic . . . be seen through their eyes. This was seen as a powerful message, and to those who are anorexic and wanting to go further into it, see[ing] these messages as motivation instead of the reverse that it was intended to be. It's funny how those [who] hate Pro-Ana unwittingly gave it a religion, isn't it? Not too many want that be known, and no wonder. Big oops, eh? Just so you know, that is their writings if you ever see and/or use it.

Myth: Pro-Ana Is Pro Death

Reality: If you [have] ever been on a Pro-Ana forum before, you will notice that a lot of the long-term members are of a normal to ever-so-slightly below normal weight range. There are very few long-termers [who] are in the medical anorexic weight range. So, true, they are thin, but in reality terms, they are, in fact, normal. In fact many of the extremely thin don't frequent pro-ed [promoting eating disorders] forums at all, they are on support forums instead. Of those [who] get to an extreme level who post pics and weights are replied back with messages of concern and pleas for them to take care of themselves and to not lose any more weight. Now you have to actually be ON the forums to know this, but those who cry out the evils do not do very good research into what they are talking about. You could say that Pro-Ana is a lot more pro-support leaning than it lets on.

Myth: Pro-Ana Is Teaching Others to Become Anorexic

Reality: You cannot "become" anorexic, it is not something you choose like a diet. Anorexia chooses you, and in the lottery of anorexia, winning is losing more than you know. It's outside factors in your own environment that make one eating disordered, not text and pictures on a website. To those [who] think you can become "ana" . . . it won't happen. You may skip a few meals, fast for a few days, but that does not make you anorexic at all. Much like a drag queen, you can look, act, talk, walk, and sing every bit like Cher . . . but you are not Cher. It's simple as that.

Myth: Pro-Ana Encourages You to Stay Anorexic

Reality: This is the touchy one. We don't encourage you to stay anorexic, but this is the biggest way in which we differ from the professional and pro-recovery sites. Instead of treating a disorder itself, Pro-Ana treats the person. We get to know the individual, what makes [her] laugh, smile, cry, and scared to see what [her] world is like through [her] eyes. See, like I said before, eating disorders are a deep-rooted problem, and there is no point trying to get rid of something that will just come back again instantly. To get rid of this, one must get to the main root and work from there. Once the root is gone, the consequences of eating disorders are that much easier to recover from . . . and the process will be a lasting one. This is why the most important part of any ed [eating disorder] forum is the journal area.

Ana Creed

I believe in Control, the only force mighty enough to bring order to the chaos that is my world.

I believe that I am the most vile, worthless and useless person ever to have existed on this planet, and that I am totally unworthy of anyone's time and attention.

I believe that other people who tell me differently must be idiots. If they could see how I really am, then they would hate me almost as much as I do.

I believe in oughts, musts and shoulds as unbreakable laws to determine my daily behavior.

I believe in perfection and strive to attain it.

I believe in salvation through trying just a bit harder than I did yesterday.

I believe in calorie counters as the inspired word of god, and memorize them accordingly.

I believe in bathroom scales as an indicator of my daily successes and failures.

I believe in hell, because I sometimes think that I'm living in it.

I believe in a wholly black and white world, the losing of weight, recrimination for sins, the abnegation of the body and a life ever fasting.

What the scale says is the most important thing.

Ana Psalm

Strict is my diet. I must not want. It maketh me to lie down at night hungry. It leadeth me past the confectioners. It trieth my willpower. It leadeth me in the paths of alteration for my figure's sake. Yea, though I walk through the aisles of the pastry department, I will buy no sweet rolls for they are fattening. The cakes and the pies, they tempt me. Before me is a table set with green beans and lettuce. I filleth my stomach with liquids, my day's quota runneth over. Surely calorie and weight charts will follow me all the days of my life, and I will dwell in the fear of the scales forever.

Ana Commandments

1. If you aren't thin you aren't attractive.

2. Being thin is more important than being healthy.

3. You must buy clothes, style your hair, take laxatives, starve yourself, do anything to make yourself look thinner.

4. Thou shall not eat without feeling guilty.

5. Thou shall not eat fattening food without punishing oneself afterwards.

6. Thou shall count calories and restrict intake accordingly.

7. What the scale says is the most important thing.

8. Losing weight is good/gaining weight is bad.

9. You can never be too thin.

10. Being thin and not eating are signs of true willpower and success.

Letter from Ana:

Allow me to introduce myself. My name, or as I am called by so-called doctors, is Anorexia. Anorexia Nervosa is my full name, but you may call me Ana. Hopefully we can become great partners. In the coming time, I will invest a lot of time in you, and I expect the same from you. In the past you have heard all of your teachers and parents talk about you. You are "so mature," "intelligent," "14 going on 45," and you possess "so much potential." Where has that gotten you, may I ask? Absolutely nowhere! You are not perfect, you do not try hard enough, furthermore you waste your time on thinking and talking with friends and drawing! Such acts of indulgence shall not be allowed in the future.

Your friends do not understand you. They are not truthful. In the past, when the insecurity has quietly gnawed away at your mind, and you asked them, "Do I look . . . fat?" and they answered, "Oh no, of course not," you knew they were lying! Only I tell the truth. Your parents, let's not even go there! You know that they love you, and care for you, but part of that is just that they are your parents and are obligated to do so. I shall tell you a secret now: Deep down inside themselves, they are disappointed with you. Their daughter, the one with so much potential, has turned into a fat, lazy, and undeserving girl.

The Scale Is All-Important

But I am about to change all that. I will expect you to drop your calorie intake and up your exercise. I will push you to the limit. You must take it because you cannot defy me! I am beginning to imbed myself into you. Pretty soon, I am with you always. I am there when you wake up in the morning and run to the scale. The numbers become both friend and enemy, and the frenzied thoughts pray for them to be lower than yesterday, last night, etc. You look into the mirror with dismay. You prod and poke at the fat that is there, and smile when you come across bone. I am there when you figure out the plan for the day: 400 calories, 2 hours exercise. I am the one figuring this out, because by now my thoughts and your thoughts are blurred together as one. I follow you throughout the day. In school, when your mind wanders, I give you something to think about. Re-count the calories for the day. It's too much. I fill your mind with thoughts of food, weight, calories, and things that are safe to think about. Because now, I am already inside of you. I am in your head, your heart, and your soul. The hunger pains you pretend not to feel is me, inside of you.

Pretty soon I am telling you not only what to do with food, but what to do ALL of the time. Smile and nod. Present yourself well. Suck in that fat stomach, dammit! God, you are such a fat cow!!!! When mealtimes come around I tell you what to do. I make a plate of lettuce seem like a feast fit for a king. Push the food around. Make it look like you've eaten something. No piece of anything . . . if you eat, all the control will be broken . . . do you WANT that?? To revert back to the fat COW you once were?? I force you to stare at magazine models. Those perfect-skinned, white-teethed, waifish models of perfection staring out at you from those glossy pages. I make you realize that you could never be them. You will always be fat, and never will you be as beautiful as they are. When you look in the mirror, I will distort the image. I will show you obesity and hideousness. I will show you a sumo wrestler where in reality there is a starving child. But you must not know this, because if you knew the truth, you might start to eat again and our relationship would come crashing down.

Sometimes you will rebel. Hopefully not often though. You will recognize the small rebellious fiber left in your body and will venture down to the dark kitchen. The cupboard door will slowly open, creaking softly. Your eyes will move over the food that I have kept at a safe distance from you. You will find your hands reaching out, lethargically, like a nightmare, through the darkness to the box of crackers. You shove them in, mechanically, not really tasting but simply relishing in the fact that you are going against me. You reach for another box, then another, then another. Your stomach will become bloated and grotesque, but you will not stop yet. And all the time I am screaming at you to stop, you fat cow, you really have no self-control, you are going to get fat.

When it is over you will cling to me again, ask me for advice because you really do not want to get fat. You broke a cardinal rule and ate, and now you want me back. I'll force you into the bathroom, onto your knees, staring into the void of the toilet bowl. Your fingers will be inserted into your throat, and, not without a great deal of pain, your food binge will come up. Over and over this is to be repeated, until you spit up blood and water and you know it is all gone. When you stand up, you will feel dizzy. Don't pass out. Stand up right now. You fat cow, you deserve to be in pain! Maybe the choice of getting rid of the guilt is different. Maybe I chose to make you take laxatives, where you sit on the toilet until the wee hours of the morning, feeling your insides cringe. Or perhaps I just make you hurt yourself, bang your head into the wall until you receive a throbbing headache. Cutting is also effective. I want you to see your blood, to see it fall down your arm, and in that split second you will realize you deserve whatever pain I give you. You are depressed, obsessed, in pain, hurting, reaching out, but no one will listen? Who cares!! You are deserving; you brought this upon yourself.

Oh, is this harsh? Do you not want this to happen to you? Am I unfair? I do things that will help you. I make it possible for you to stop thinking of emotions that cause you stress. Thoughts of anger, sadness, desperation, and loneliness can cease because I take them away and fill your head with the methodic calorie counting. I take away your struggle to fit in with kids your age, the struggle of trying to please everyone as well. Because now, I am your only friend, and I am the only one you need to please. I have a weak spot. But we must not tell anyone. If you decide to fight back, to reach out to someone and tell them about how I make you live, all hell will break lose. No one must find out, no one can crack this shell that I have covered you with. I have created you, this thin, perfect, achieving child. You are mine and mine alone. Without me, you are nothing. So do not fight back. When others comment, ignore them. Take it [in] stride, forget about them, forget about everyone that tries to take me away. I am your greatest asset, and I intend to keep it that way.

Sincerely,

Ana

Dear Ana:

I offer you my soul, my heart, and my bodily functions. I give you all my earthly possessions.

I seek your wisdom, your faith, and your feather weight. I pledge to obtain the ability to float, to lower my weight to the single digits, I pledge to stare into space, to fear food, and to see obese images in the mirror. I will worship you and pledge to be a faithful servant until death does us part.

If I cheat on you and procreate with Ronald McDonald, Dave Thomas [Wendy's], the colonel [KFC], or that cute little dog [Taco Bell], I will kneel over my toilet and thrust my fingers deep in my throat and pray for your forgiveness.

Please Ana, don't give up on me. I'm so weak, I know, but only . . . with your strength inside me will I become a woman worthy of love and respect. I'm begging for you not to give up, I'm pleading with my shallow breaths and my pale skin. I bleed for you, suffer leg pains, headaches, and fainting spells. My love for you makes me dizzy and confused. I don't know whether I'm coming or going. Men run when they see the love I have for you and never return. But they aren't important to me, all that's important is that you love me.

If you stay with me, I will worship you daily, I will run miles a day, come rain, snow, bitter cold, or searing heat. I will run from the pain and in fright. I will do 1,000 sit ups a day and lie to my family about what I eat and how I feel. I will stop weeping when I feel your warm arms embrace my shivering body. I will numb the hunger pains with razor blades and your strength.

Today, I renew our friendship and resolve to be faithful to you year long, life long. I begin each year with a 3-day fast in honor of you. If you give me the strength to fade away, I will love you and worship you forever.

When I'm finally faded to nothing, when you've given me the gift of ending this torturous life, I will float on to the next world and be thin and beautiful payment for my undying love for you in this world.

I ask only one more thing [of] you, please Ana, remove me from this hell, from this world ASAP. Please take away this hatred for my pain and allow me to be free and light.

Love Always,

(Insert Name Here)

13

Anorexia Is a False Religion

Courtney Martin

Courtney Martin is the author of Perfect Girls, Starving Daughters: How the Quest for Perfection is Harming Young Women. *She works as a journalist and is a senior correspondent for* The American Prospect Online.

Fashion models, dysfunctional families, and the dieting industry all contribute to rising numbers of anorexics, but a lack of spirituality is at the core of the illness. Divinity has been replaced by thinness and spirituality supplanted by the ambition to succeed in a money-driven world.

Worried talk about the next generation of high-achieving, health-neglecting "perfect girls" is everywhere.

Girls Inc. just published the results of its depressing, nationwide survey called "The Supergirl Dilemma," which reveals that girls' obsession with thinness has gotten significantly worse in the past six years. Despite the efforts of ... Dove's Campaign for Real Beauty—well-intentioned, though undeniably market-driven—and Love Your Body Day events sweeping every school from San Francisco to Syracuse, 90 percent of teenage girls think they are overweight today, compared with 24 percent in 1995, according to a recent ELLEgirl survey.

Anorexia Is a Multifaceted Problem

So what gives? Is it our celebrity-obsessed, extreme-makeover culture? Is it the newest version of the age-old story of dysfunctional family relationships? Is it peer pressure—mean girls

Courtney Martin, "For Girls Who Hate Their Bodies: A Spiritual Crisis," *The Christian Science Monitor*, April 24, 2007. © 2007 The Christian Science Monitor. Reproduced by permission of the author.

critiquing one another's every lunchtime indiscretion? Is it the $30-billion-a-year diet industry?

It is, in truth, all of the above. But there is also another profoundly important—yet little-noticed—dynamic at work in the anxious, achievement-oriented lives of America's perfect girls: They have a sometimes deadly, often destructive, lack of faith.

We were raised largely without a fundamental sense of divinity.

So many perfect girls were raised entirely without organized religion, and the majority of the rest of us—I reluctantly admit to my own membership in the perfect girl club—experienced "spirituality" only in the form of mandatory holiday services with a big-haired grandmother or unconscionably elaborate and expensive bat mitvah [Jewish coming-of-age ceremony] parties, where everything but the Torah [the first five books of the Hebrew scripture] is emphasized.

Overlay our dearth of spiritual exploration with our excess of training in ambition—never mind SAT prep courses; today, even community service is linked to college application brownie points—and you have a generation of godless girls. We were raised largely without a fundamental sense of divinity. In fact, our worth in the world has always been tied to our looks, grades, and gifts—not the amazing miracle of mere existence.

In this climate, we feel perpetually called to perfect our own "body projects"—the term used by historian Joan Jacob Brumberg. Thinness and achievement stand in for the qualities of kindness and humility. We think that our perfect bodies—not God's grace or good works—will get us into heaven. We have no deeply held sense of our own divinity, so we chase after some unattainable ideal. Perfect girls, as a result, feel they are never enough. Never disciplined enough. Never accomplished enough. Never thin enough.

False Gods

The worst of this can be seen in the frightening websites that purport to be support groups for girls with anorexia and bulimia. Such sites claim that these two disorders are a religion, not a disease, and pray to false gods named after them: Ana and Mia. Though highly deluded and dangerously ill, girls who frequent these sites have taken the black hole at their centers and filled it with an obsessive faith in the power and purity of thinness. In essence, they are crying out to our godless culture, showing us just how damaged a child can be who is thrown to the wolves of advertising and amoral media without any spiritual armor.

I'm not calling for a return to conservative religion or restricting dogma. I'm envisioning an inspired movement toward community where girls are nourished with dinner-table conversations about the values of kindness and charity; where girls undergoing puberty are encouraged to embrace the miraculous, complex, and perfectly imperfect bodies they possess; and where girls can find inspiration—not condemnation—in religious texts.

It is we, all of us, who have the power to resurrect a society that values spirit above skinniness.

For starters, the Bible has something to teach the perfect girl who calculates beauty in terms of pounds and dress sizes: "Your beauty should not come from outward adornment. . . . Instead, it should be that of your inner self, the unfading beauty of a gentle and quiet spirit, which is of great worth in God's sight" (I Peter 3:3,4, New International Version).

Loving the Imperfect Self

And Buddha, the man often portrayed as blissful with his belly, has a paradigm-shifting message for the average American woman accustomed to self-hate: "You, yourself, as much as anybody in the entire universe, deserve your love and affection."

In the age of the skeletal celebrity-filled *US Weekly* and shrill sound bite commentators such as [conservative commentator] Ann Coulter, these are the kinds of deep reflections and recommendations we perfect girls need most.

A supermom of an elite college hopeful told *New York Times* reporter Sara Rimer, "You just hope your child doesn't have anorexia of the soul." While she is spot-on in her fears, she seems woefully shortsighted about her responsibilities. It is we, all of us, who have the power to resurrect a society that values spirit above skinniness. We have to start doing it—one prayer, one family hike, one heart-to-heart discussion about what really matters—at a time.

Organizations to Contact

The editors have compiled the following list of organizations concerned with the issues debated in this book. The descriptions are derived from materials provided by the organizations. All have publications or information available for interested readers. The list was compiled on the date of publication of the present volume; the information provided here may change. Readers need to remember that many organizations take several weeks or longer to respond to inquiries.

Alliance for Eating Disorders Awareness (The Alliance)
PO Box 13155, North Palm Beach, FL   33408-3155
(561) 841-0900
Web site: www.eatingdisorderinfo.org

The Alliance seeks to establish easily accessible programs across the nation that allow children and young adults the opportunity to learn about eating disorders. It provides information about anorexia nervosa on its Web site and also makes a checklist available for anyone who seeks to establish whether a friend or family member might be afflicted.

American Academy of Child and Adolescent Psychiatry (AACAP)
3615 Wisconsin Ave. NW, Washington, DC   20016-3007
(202) 966-7300 • fax: (202) 966-2891
Web site: www.aacap.org

The American Academy of Child and Adolescent Psychiatry is a national professional medical association dedicated to treating and improving the quality of life for children, adolescents, and families affected by their disorders. AACAP publishes interviews and videos on its Web site, as well as the information series *Facts for Families*, and articles such as "Teenagers with Eating Disorders."

American Dietetic Association (ADA)
216 West Jackson Blvd., Chicago, IL 60606-6995
(800) 877-1600
Web site: www.eatright.org

The American Dietetic Association is the world's largest organization of food and nutrition professionals. ADA seeks to improve the nation's health and advance the profession of dietetics through research, education, and advocacy. Articles, research findings, and the *Journal of the American Dietetic Association* can be accessed online.

American Psychological Association (APA)
750 First Street NE, Washington, DC 20002-4242
(202) 336-5500 • fax: (202) 336-5708
E-mail: public.affairs@apa.org
Web site: www.apa.org

The APA aims to "advance psychology as a science, as a profession, and as a means of promoting human welfare." It produces numerous publications, including the monthly journal *American Psychologist*, the monthly newspaper *APA Monitor*, and the quarterly *Journal of Abnormal Psychology*.

Eating Disorders Coalition (EDC)
609 10th Street NE, Suite #1, Washington, DC 20002
(202) 543-3842
Web site: www.eatingdisorderscoalition.org

The EDC promotes, at the federal level, further investment in the healthy development of children at risk for eating disorders, recognition of eating disorders as a public health priority, and commitment to effective prevention and evidence-based, accessible treatment of these disorders. The EDC Web site makes available to the public news and information.

Multi-service Eating Disorders Association (MEDA)
92 Pearl Street, Newton, MA 02458
(866) 343-MEDA (6332)

E-mail: info@medainc.org
Web site: www.medainc.org

MEDA is a nonprofit organization dedicated to the prevention and treatment of eating disorders and disordered eating. MEDA's mission is to prevent the continuing spread of eating disorders through educational awareness and early detection. MEDA serves as a support network and a resource for clinicians, educators, and the general public.

National Association of Anorexia Nervosa and Associated Disorders (ANAD)

PO Box 640, Naperville, IL 60566
(630) 577-1333
Web site: www.anad.org

The ANAD is a nonprofit corporation that seeks to prevent and alleviate the problems of eating disorders, especially anorexia nervosa, bulimia nervosa, and binge-eating disorder. ANAD helps educate the general public and professionals in the health care field to be more aware of illnesses relating to eating disorders and methods of treatment. Facts about anorexia and how people can help prevent it are made available on the Web site.

National Eating Disorders Association (NEDA)

603 Stewart Street, Suite 803, Seattle, WA 98101
(206) 382-3587 • fax: (206) 292-9890
Web site: www.nationaleatingdisorders.org

NEDA promotes the awareness and prevention of eating disorders by encouraging self-esteem. It provides free and low-cost educational information on eating disorders and their prevention. NEDA also provides educational outreach programs and training for schools and universities, and provides treatment referrals to persons suffering from anorexia, bulimia, and binge-eating disorder and to people concerned with body image and weight issues.

Bibliography

Books

Carrie Arnold   *Next to Nothing: A Firsthand Account of One Teenager's Experience with an Eating Disorder.* New York, NY: Oxford University Press, 2007.

Ruth Bjorkland   *Eating Disorders.* New York, NY: Marshall Cavendish Benchmark, 2006.

Cynthia Bulik   *Crave: Why You Binge Eat and How to Stop.* New York, NY: Walker & Company, 2009.

Carolyn Costin   *The Eating Disorders Sourcebook.* New York, NY: McGraw-Hill, 2007.

Sheryle Cruse   *Thin Enough: My Spiritual Journey Through the Living Death of an Eating Disorder.* Birmingham, AL: New Hope, 2006.

Shannon Cutts   *Beating Ana: How to Outsmart Your Eating Disorder & Take Your Life Back.* Deerfield Beach, FL: HCI, 2009.

Cheryl Dellasega   *The Starving Family: Caregiving Mothers and Fathers Share Their Eating Disorder Wisdom.* Fredonia, WI: Champion Press, 2005.

Valerie Elsbree   *Eating Disorders: A Guide for Families and Children.* Jupiter, FL: Merit Publishing International, 2008.

Leslie Goldman   *Locker Room Diaries: The Naked Truth About Women, Body Image, and Re-Imagining the "Perfect" Body.* Cambridge, MA: Da Capo Long Life, 2006.

Christine Halse   *Inside Anorexia: The Experiences of Girls and Their Families.* London, UK: Jessica Kingsley Publishers, 2008.

Jeanne Albronda Heaton   *Talking to Eating Disorders: Simple Ways to Support Someone with Anorexia, Bulimia, Binge Eating or Body Image Issues.* New York: New American Library, 2005.

Karen Koenig   *The Rules of "Normal" Eating: A Commonsense Aproach for Dieters, Overeaters, Undereaters, Emotional Eaters and Everyone in Between.* Carlsbad, CA: Gurze Books, 2005.

Gerri Freid Kramer   *The Truth About Eating Disorders.* New York: Facts On File, 2005.

Sandra Augustyn Lawton, ed.   *Eating Disorders Information for Teens: Health Tips About Anorexia, Bulimia, Binge Eating and Other Eating Disorders.* Detroit, MI: Omnigraphics, 2005.

Michael Levine   *The Prevention of Eating Problems and Eating Disorders: Theory, Research and Practice.* Mahwah, NJ: Lawrence Erlbaum Associates, 2006.

Aimee Lui

Gaining: The Truth About Life After Eating Disorders. New York: Warner, 2007.

Margo Maine

The Body Myth: Adult Women and the Pressure to Be Perfect. Hoboken, NJ: John Wiley & Sons, 2005.

Susan Nolen-Hoeksema

Eating, Drinking, Overthinking: The Toxic Triangle of Food, Alcohol and Depression—and How Women Can Break Free. New York: Henry Holt, 2006.

P. Scott Richards

Spiritual Approaches in the Treatment of Women with Eating Disorders. Washington, DC. American Psychological Association, 2007.

Margie Ryerson

Appetite for Life: Inspiring Stories of Recovery from Anorexia, Bulimia and Compulsive Overeating. Lincoln, NE: iUniverse, 2005.

Joyce Shannon, ed.

Eating Disorders Sourcebook. Omnigraphics 2006.

Lori Smolin

Nutrition and Eating Disorders. Philadelphia, PA: Chelsea House, 2005.

Periodicals

Clive Barnes

"The Weight of Bodies: The Scales of Fatness Vary from Era to Era, Not to Mention Person to Person," *Dance Magazine,* July 2008.

Fiona Bawdon   "No Model for Girls: Controversy over 'Size Zero' Models Is No Longer Confined to the Fashion Industry. There Is Now Solid Evidence That Images of Super-Thin Celebrities in the Media Have a Direct Effect on the Well-Being of Teenagers," *New Statesman*, October 1, 2007.

Birmingham Post   "Jockeys Are the Size Zeroes of Sport," March 10, 2008.

Deborah Blum   "Twin Fates: Sharing the Womb with a Brother May Influence a Girl's Development," *Science News*, May 10, 2008.

Bruce Bower   "Starved for Assistance: Coercion Finds a Place in the Treatment of Two Eating Disorders," *Science News*, January 20, 2007.

Bruce Bower   "Wasting Away: Prozac Loses Promise as Anorexia Nervosa Fighter," *Science News*, June 17, 2006.

Catherine Cook-Cottone   "The Attuned Representation Model for Primary Prevention of Eating Disorders: An Overview for School Psychologists," *Psychology in the Schools*, 2006.

Laura Hensley Choate and Alan Schwitzer   "Mental Health Counseling Responses to Eating-Related Concerns in Young Adult Women: A Prevention and Treatment Continuum," *Journal of Mental Health Counseling*, 2009.

Daily Mail	"Anorexic at the Age of 6; More and More Girls—and Boys—Have Eating Disorders Before Their Teens," March 27, 2007.
Evening Standard	"'There Are No Size Zeros on the London Catwalk,'" February 12, 2007.
Annie Kelly	"A Tiny Step for Womankind: Argentina Is Fighting the Fashionistas with a Law Against Micro-Sized Clothing," *New Statesman*, March 27, 2006.
Mail on Sunday	"The Websites That Encourage Anorexia," January 29, 2006.
The Mirror	"Anorexia: It's a Family Thing," November 12, 2008.
David Luc Nguyen	"Wasting Away: What's Driving Young Gay Men to Starve, Binge, and Purge?" *Advocate*, September 26, 2006.
Wendy Oliver	"Body Image in the Dance Class: Dance Educators Can and Should Help Their Dancers Develop and Maintain a Positive Body Image," *Journal of Physical Education, Recreation & Dance*, May/June 2008.
Washington Times	"Eating Disorders Rife on Campus; Few Treated for Problem Ranked No. 3," September 28, 2006.
Frances Wilson	"Women on the Verge," *New Statesman*, February 18, 2008.

Shelli Yoder   "Perfect Girls, Starving Daughters: The Frightening New Normalcy of Hating Your Bod," *Christian Century*, January 15, 2008.

Index